S0-BRN-973

SANCTIFICATION BY THE TRUTH.

SANCTIFICATION

BY THE

TRUTH:

SERMONS PREACHED FOR THE MOST PART IN WESTMINSTER ABBEY.

BY

BASIL WILBERFORCE, D.D.,

Archdeacon of Westminster;
Chaplain to the House of Commons;
Select Preacher before the University of Oxford.

NEW YORK:
E. P. DUTTON & Co.,

AND

LONDON:
ELLIOT STOCK.

PREFACE.

GOD'S TRUTH.

THE author of the book of Proverbs (xxiii. 3) bids us " buy the truth." He suggests apparently that, inasmuch as every attainment, knowledge, accomplishment is bought at the price of application and patience, it is not otherwise with the most momentous of all considerations, the gradual self-revelation of the Infinite mind to the human understanding.

The truth, as a final discovery, exists in no department of knowledge. The ascertained truths of this material universe, bought by the physical investigation of one generation at the price of patient labour, are transcended by the truths which the investigation of another generation will buy at a still higher price. It is the same in connection with truths concerning the nature, and relation to creation of the Infinite Originator, for " God's truth " is not a final attainment, but an ever-increasing illumination ; it is the secret inward reality ; the cause, the meaning, the relation of everything ; it is that spiritual realization of conscious life in God towards which the human soul ever evolves throughout eternity.

> Dark is the soul's eye ; yet how it strives and battles
> Through the impenetrable gloom to fix
> That Master light, *the secret truth of things*,
> Which is the body of the Infinite God.

The sermons in this volume represent nothing more than the aspirations of a humble truth-seeker, whose constant prayer is, " Lead me in Thy truth, and teach me : for Thou art the God of my salvation ; on Thee do I wait all the day " (Ps. xxv. 5—Bible Version).

CONTENTS.

		PAGE
1.	GOD'S TRUTH	1
2.	LIMITING THE HOLY ONE	12
3.	THE AWAKENING	25
4.	MOTHERHOOD IN GOD	40
5.	THE ORIGIN OF MAN	51
6.	WHEAT AND TARES	65
7.	OUGHT THE CLERGY TO CRITICIZE THE BIBLE?	74
8.	THE OBLIGATION OF THE SABBATH ...	85
9.	NELSON AND TRAFALGAR	97
10.	THE BISHOP OF LONDON'S FUND	108
11.	JOINT HEIRS WITH CHRIST	119
12.	VIRTUE	129
13.	KNOWLEDGE	138
14.	SELF-CONTROL	150
15.	PATIENCE	160
16.	GODLINESS	170
17.	BROTHERLY KINDNESS	180
18.	OUR FATHER WHICH ART IN HEAVEN ...	189
19.	HALLOWED BE THY NAME	202
20.	THY KINGDOM COME	213
21.	THY WILL BE DONE...	227
22.	GIVE US THIS DAY OUR DAILY BREAD ...	240
23.	FORGIVE US OUR TRESPASSES	255
24.	LEAD US NOT INTO TEMPTATION	266
25.	THINE IS THE KINGDOM	277

GOD'S TRUTH.

A Thought for a New Year.

———

"Sanctify them by Thy truth."—*John* xvii. 7.

ST. PAUL, in Eph. iv. 21-22, defines and explains this mystic utterance of our Lord : " If so be that ye have been taught the truth as it is in Jesus . . . that ye put off the old nature and be renewed in the spirit of your mind." This, then, is God's truth, the truth as it is in Jesus, "the truth that sanctifies"; that there is a renewing power within man, a pure and Eternal germ which, when recognised and co-operated with, will outgrow the carnal nature, and by the steady, gradual, continual conquest of the lower life by the higher, perfect human character, and conform it to the image of the Christ.

"Sanctify them by Thy truth." The words suggest an appropriate supplication to be interchanged at the beginning of a New Year. Obviously we cannot use the words as authoritatively as they were used by our Lord. The Greek words attributed to our Lord by the

author of the fourth Gospel imply a demand
rather than a supplication. " I will," He says,
" I will that where I am there shall they be
also." It is only the ideal human being, the
Divine Humanity, He who knows as a fact of
experience that He and the Father are essentially one, who can thus use them, and there
has only been One thus perfect. But we, who
have reached just the threshold of understanding
the meaning of intercession, which is the divine
in man reaching forth to and blending with the
universal Divine, and setting free influences
which without such blending would be inert,
we can use them in the same mental attitude,
though without the same conscious authority.

His truth, God's truth, easy words to utter ;
they even constitute a too common expletive,
but what do they really imply ?   The distinction
between God's truth on the material and intellectual plane, and God's truth on the intuitive
and spiritual plane is incalculable.   The first is
a fixed point with finality ; the second is an
acquisition, increasing in proportion to recep-
tivity, which has not, and never will have,
finality.   The first is ascertained fact, discovered
by the investigator, which enables man to form
a right judgment in the perplexities of life ;
and ascertained fact, whether of physiology,
history, mathematics, or morals, is God's truth
just because it is true, and it affects the life and
purposes of man in the direction of justice and

freedom. The second, which is on the intuitive and spiritual plane, is an increasing assurance of certain inferences concerning the Generative Love-Spirit called God, which stimulate the inner springs of action and emotion, and bind us to the invisible. And to this experience there is not, and there never can be, finality. God's truth, therefore, on this plane, the " truth as it is in Jesus," is a gradual unfolding of the soul's hidden capacities, accompanied by new and ever enlarging conceptions of the Infinite Originator, with an ever-increasing sense of rest and security in the Soul of the Universe. Has not this been the experience of most of us ? Has not our conception of the Infinite constantly expanded ? Can we not echo the thought in those lines :—

> God is God from the creation,
> Truth alone is man's salvation,
> But the God that now you worship
> Soon shall be your God no more ;
> For the soul in its unfolding,
> Evermore its thought re-moulding,
> Learns more truly in its progress
> How to love and to adore.

Yes, the God that now we worship differs surprisingly from earlier conceptions, which once satisfied us. God has not changed, it is we who have changed ; our eyes are getting keener, and this enlargement of truth ought to sanctify ; for upward thought, Godward aspiration, spiritual experience, free the soul from pessimism, check the fire of passion, strengthen the capacity for endurance, elevate the aim and scope of life. I ask you to look back over the thought-path you have traversed in your effort to follow the gleam. Once we were Deists, with, superadded to our Deism, an intricate theological scheme or plan by which we could reach the far-distant God we worshipped. Since we mentally de-localised God and took Him out of limitations, we have gradually entered into the assurance that the whole universe, like Moses' bush, is aflame with His Presence, that His ceaselessly reproducing generative power throbs in every blade, uplifts every seed, abides in every man, and therefore that we, as offspring of the In-finite Spirit, are essentially as indestructible as God Himself. This truth came pushing its way through rigid traditions and early prejudices and dogmatic limitations, and its very immensity caused at times a sense of vagueness. When this sense of vagueness supervenes, the heart hankers after the old traditions and limitations, and men are inclined to think that they have lost something. They have lost nothing. Every valued tradition of Catholic Christendom is theirs still, only now it is full of meaning, now it glows and shines. Our creed is there, but now we can reconcile it to our reason. The Incarnation is there, not now as the unphilosophical limita-tion of a universal truth to a single Personality, but as the perfect manifestation in a single unique Personality of a divine immanence and sonship, which is the attribute of humanity as a whole. It was thus that we slowly delivered ourselves from certain cherished limitations which are still the battle-cries of opposing schools of thought, and we delivered ourselves without losing a single item of what was true and inspired in any of them.

It is profitable to review the steps by which this sanctifying truth, this " truth as it is in Jesus," unfolded. First you believed on authority, and belief on authority, though a useful element in social order, is not personal faith. Then, probably, you hunted for the Infinite Originator by the method of philosophic induction based on the results of scientific research which you studied. If you did, you found Him ; that is, you arrived at the point where the affirmation of an originating mind behind the universe became to you intellectually a logical necessity, and you were constrained to acknowledge that throughout all the material forces of nature there was but One Majestic Elemental Principle of Life, and you naturally proceeded, by an orderly sequence of thought, to predicate an all-creating, all-sustaining Intelligence, responsible for everything, and though unable to define, and incapable of predicating personality in the human sense to what you had found, you were face to face with God, the Infinite Universal Parent Spirit ; you had felt after Him

and you had found Him, and though He was too
vast for you to know, you perceived that you
were His offspring. But transcendent as this
discovery is, it does not represent all that is
meant by "the truth as it is in Jesus." This
discovery was not made for the first time by
Herbert Spencer and Huxley and Tyndall, it
was made by all the Eastern thinkers two thousand years before Christ. To this point the
pagan poet, Cleanthes, whose words St. Paul
quoted on Mars Hill, had led his followers.
There is nothing new in the discovery of what
Professor Huxley called "the passionless imper-
sonality that science everywhere discovers behind the thin veil of phenomena." But the
unlocalised Infinite Originator is not knowable
in His entirety as human hearts crave to know
Him. The Agnostics are right there. Much,
very much, you can know about Him as He
expresses Himself in infinite diversity in all
visible things; but His tenderness, His intimacy,
His sympathy, His characteristics that are reflected in us, we cannot know through His self-
expression in nature. Has He revealed them to
us to whom the fulness of time has come?
Charles Kingsley once unfolded to me in a
private conversation his mental experience on
arriving at this point. He followed sequences
logically. It is all in his novel "Hypatia." If
all phenomena, he reasoned, are expressions of
the One Intelligence, God, and if humanity is

the highest of these expressions, then the noblest specimen of humanity is the most perfect expression of God, and, by consequence, while still human, wholly Divine. Therefore, Jesus is God; not because the Council of Nicœa says He is, but by inherent necessity. And though Jesus is God under a limitation, God is at the same time in all things, as the Eastern thinkers and Cleanthes taught, but He is specially knowable, discoverable, intelligible, adorable in Jesus. This, if men would understand it, was the Creed of Christ; not a maze of theological subtleties, but a single clear philosophical proposition. God, He taught, is Spirit; the conscious immanent energy of the universe; though we and that creative Spirit are inseverable, we cannot form any clear mental conception of Him. Therefore, His attitude towards us, and the characteristics of His nature that we most need, and that will most sooth and attract us, are embodied in one specific specimen of the race for our study and observation. And so He said, " Ye believe in God, believe also in Me," which, being interpreted, is, " Ye believe in the Universal Soul, believe in the self-manifestation of the human characteristics of the Universal Soul in Me," for " he that hath seen Me " hath, so far as is possible or profitable for the finite soul, " seen the Father."

But even this is not all of the " truth as it is in Jesus;" there was nothing cramped or exclu-

sive in the Creed of the Christ; He emphatically
avoided limiting to His single Personality the
immanent divine nature which was so conspicu-
ously, so perfectly manifested in Himself. He
claimed it for humanity as a whole. He made it
clear that He was humanity at its climax, and
He taught that what He was all men could be,
and were ultimately predestined to be, for that
His nature, His spirit, the divine sonship so
transcendently uniquely embodied in Him, was
potential and dormant in every man, and that,
when awakened, yielded to, co-operated with,
it would energise within all, growing out the
animal nature, renewing the ideal humanity in
each one, until each in his turn attained unto
the "measure of the stature of the fulness of
Christ." This I understand to be "the truth
as it is in Jesus"; the truth that Jesus is the
manifestor of the humanity in God and the
divinity in man ; and holding firmly this esoteric
philosophic truth you have not lost one proposition of the creed of Christendom, and you
can adore Jesus without the slightest intellectual
separation of God from Jesus, or Jesus from
humanity, and you know what He meant when
He said, "I in them and Thou in Me, that they
may be made perfect in One."

One word of application. "Sanctify them by
Thy truth" is a prayer to the Universal Soul in
one aspect, it is a command of universal obligation addressed to every believer in another

aspect. Have you arrived at a higher, nobler view of human destiny ? Have you emancipated your God conception from limitations ? Is it conceivable that you may lock up that truth in your bosom for your own delectation ? It will burn and torment you if you do. It is yours in trust for others. Sanctify others with that truth that you have got. How ? Not by bitterly controverting other people's rudimentary conceptions ; rudimentary conceptions are sufficient for rudimentary minds. Not even always by heroically storming the strongholds of the empire of all that unsanctifies ; it is given to some, but not many, to do this. The sanctification of others by your truth is effected by being rather than doing. Dr. Martineau well said that having, doing, and being are the three distinctive characteristics of humanity, and the greatest of these is being. Some men are eminent for what they have, others for what they achieve, others for what they are ; to get good is animal, to do good is human, to be good is divine. And the greatest of these is to be good. Why is this ? Because good and evil are not abstractions outside man, but forces within man. And just as every member of the race who is living for the flesh, ruled by the appetites, dominated by self, contributes to increase the aggregate of the pollution of humanity, so every member of the race who quietly lives the higher life, though he does not possess much, and cannot do much,

by just being pure in his life, sweet in his temper,
devout in his spirit, self-controlled in his actions,
frequent in prayer, slow to anger and of great
kindness, contributes to create that atmosphere
of godliness which re-animates, uplifts, inspires
the human race. It is God's eternal counsel that
the mass of moral evil in the world shall be
transformed by the secret, silent, almost unobserved power of good. There is nothing in nature
more striking than a great glacier, except, perhaps, a great cataract. And a glacier is a
cataract petrified ; the Mer de Glace is Niagara
frozen. A huge tumbling torrent as still as
death, but with the form and appearance of
violent ·motion. But, still as it is, it is yet
moving. God's chemistry is converting it from
a death-dealing monster into a source of fertility
and life. But what moves it ? What causes it
to slide down the mountain gorge and issue in
fertilizing rivers ? Not the sun, for it moves no
faster in summer than in winter. It is the
gradual radiation of the unobserved indwelling
heat of the earth, melting its under side, that
moves the glacier. Not otherwise is it with the
heart-freezing moral glacier that we call evil.
What overpowers evil in this world ? The quiet
outbreathing of the heart warmth of thousands
of believing, trusting, praying, pure living, right
thinking men and women keep the glacier moving,
turning everywhere evil into good. The thought,
then, with which to commence a new year is

this : How much are we contributing in our individual lives to the melting of the glacier of moral evil ? Are we each one doing our part in our, perhaps, modest sphere of duty ? Be good and you will do good. Live the truth and you will sanctify by the truth. One brave protest against the prevailing conceptions of the character of God ; one quiet, gentle answer given under great provocation ; one failing heart sweetly comforted for the sake of Him who indwells humanity ; one high principle quietly asserted at some cost to yourself ; and, so extensive and so incalculable is the power of influence, you will have contributed your warmth to the underside of the glacier ; you will have made the world perceptibly better, and in your own person you will have fulfilled the inspired command :

" SANCTIFY THEM BY THY TRUTH."

LIMITING THE HOLY ONE.

" They limited the Holy One of Israel."—*Psalm* lxxviii. 41
(Bible Version).

THE festival of the Epiphany, which gives
their name to the several Sundays between
Christmas and Septuagesima in the Calendar of
the Church, is essentially the festival of the
abolition of limitations of time, space, or nation-
ality from the Holy One of our Israel, the protest
of the Spirit of God against all sectarian narrowness, Calvinistic exclusiveness, and cramped, un-
worthy conceptions of Divine Love. Epiphany is
the inspired commentary upon this accusation of
the Psalmist against the Jewish people : " They
limited the Holy One of Israel." It is the asser-
tion of the fundamental fact of the Christian
revelation that no race, or nation, or individual,
or Church can dare to monopolize the protection,
the love, the accessibility of the Universal Spirit.
For Epiphany commemorates the fact that the
first to recognise the new era in the religious
history of the world, the first to worship God
revealed in flesh in the infant Jesus, were
strangers to the covenant of promise, astrologers

from Parthia, outside the bounds of this favoured race who " limited the Holy One of Israel." Judaism received the sentence of its coming abolition from the lips of its greatest poet-prophet whenever this Psalm was chanted in the Levitical service, but prejudice blinded them, and the result was inevitable. Air cut off from the universal air, tightly enclosed, and breathed again and again by the same lungs becomes incapable of supporting life ; men die if they limit the life-giver of their bodies. The majesty of All Fatherhood, cut off from universal humanity, enclosed in narrow shibboleths, selfishly mono-polized by a few, becomes incapable of sup-porting spirituality ; the moral life is fatally im-poverished. Exclusiveness asphyxiates churches ; men spiritually die because they have " limited the Holy One of Israel."

The history of the theological, moral, and intellectual progress of this world is one un-ceasing witness that nothing dies so hard as this error. The Psalmist in this short sentence, " They limited the Holy One of Israel," has placed his finger upon a moral failing which down the ages has incapacitated nations, churches, individuals. Over many an arrested development, over many a Church impotent for reform, over many a mind wandering in unbelief, over many a nation at war with a brother nation, over many a life restless, vacillating, unhappy, the Psalmist's sentence might be written as an epitaph, " They limited the Holy One of Israel."

Intellectual limitation, for example, is the history of nearly all scientific unbelief. Deep is the obligation of religion to scientific research ; the patient pursuit of sequences leading up to the unity and intelligence of the primal cause, the discovery of the invariability of the laws that govern all forms of life, have widened our views of God and added new beauty and new sublimity to Nature. But why are some scientific men agnostics ? Because they tie down the infinite reason that they have discovered to the physical laws which they acknowledge it has made ; they " limit the Holy One "; they refuse to follow out the higher problems suggested ; and to stop where they stop is to make life an uncertainty and death a leap in the dark. To refuse to limit, to follow unfalteringly, is to acknowledge with the late Professor W. B. Carpenter, the great mental physiologist, that it is as illogical to deny a God in nature as to deny a mind in man ; or to confess, as Sir Andrew Clarke, that prince of physicians, confessed in Exeter Hall, that it was impossible for him not to be a Christian unless he denied his reason.

Again, ecclesiastical limitation is the starting point of sectarian animosity, civil war in the Churches, cruel persecution. Men have eagerly propagated the view of the Gospel taught by the particular community through which they received their spiritual convictions. To do this

is natural and it is right ; but they have imagined
that they alone, as a religious system, possessed
a monopoly of the Fatherhood of God revealed
by the Incarnation of the Christ, and they have
cursed, persecuted, and unchurched all that were
without. The fire and sword of past days, the
disabilities of Roman Catholics and Nonconformists of later times, and the miserable narrowness of some so-called religious newspapers of
to-day, through the columns of which rings the
cry, " The temple of the Lord, the temple of the
Lord, the temple of the Lord are we," these
are the echoes of the old sin, they " limited the
Holy One of Israel." And the sin involves the
same consequences as of old ; loss of spirituality,
worldliness, impotence against evil, the water of
life stagnating in our cisterns while " darkest
England " cries for light. Epiphany reveals
Illimitable Fatherhood. " Our Father which art
in heaven " is not your monopoly or mine. His
Christ is universal. He is not one man, but the
Archetype of all men. He is the vital element in
which all souls have their being ; shut Him up
in one nation, one Church, one creed, and He
has not room to breathe. The adoration of the
Magi may teach us that while we value highly
and use constantly every privilege of our Church,
it has no monopoly of God. Believe, teach, live
the doctrine of All Fatherhood, and the world
will need no other theology. The jarring hos-
tilities of rival sects would die if men would cease
to " limit the Holy One of Israel."

Once more. Theological limitation of the in-extinguishable purpose of the Holy One of Israel, with regard to the humanity for which He is responsible, is the sure promoter of pessimism, the parent of atheism, and the origin of despair. We look out at our great cities and shudder at the degradation of the multitudes that swarm in the slums ; we know that nine-tenths of them are born hereditarily disposed to vice and indolence, and condemned by their environment to temptation from their childhood. If we are Christians, we stretch out our arms so far as they will reach to help the needy, comfort the sorrowful, restore the lost. The patient administration of God's inexhaustible remedy for sin is blessed to many, but thousands die unreached, unawakened. Sent into the world by a powerful will not their own, without choosing their own surroundings, after a short life of privation and squalor they are gone out of the world. Whither ? What awaits them beyond the grave ? The answer of the optimist is : The Holy One of Israel has said, " All souls are mine "; He has said, "All nations whom Thou hast made shall come and worship Thee, O Lord, and shall glorify Thy name ; they shall remember themselves, and be turned to the Lord "; He has said this, and we know that He will accomplish it, though methods, times, and seasons are His own. Surely it is the old sin condemned by the Psalmist when men interpose their barriers and dare to

say to the Holy One of Israel, No, thus far shalt
Thou go and no farther.　They forget that there
is One who says, "All power is given unto Me,
both in heaven and on earth "; that is, power
over all wills, all acts, all thoughts, all spirits,
all living, and all dead.　" I am come," said He,
" not to condemn the world, but that the world
through Me should be saved."　"Ah," reply the
limiters of the Holy One, " 'all' must be taken
in a lesser sense ; it refers only to a few, and only
to this life.　Now is the day of salvation.　He is
the Saviour now ; He will be the destroyer hereafter "; and, as if in solemn contradiction to
this criminal limitation, sound forth the glorious
words : " I am the Lord, I change not "; " Jesus
Christ, the same yesterday, to-day, and for
ever."　And in that " for ever " it never ceases
to be " now."　Over this " gospel " of a defeated Saviour, a bereaved God, and a more than
half empty heaven, what motto more appropriate to inscribe than the Psalmist's epitaph,
" They limited the Holy One of Israel."

Is this, think you, an unpractical line of
thought for daily life ?　Do you imagine that as
we are perhaps not tempted to ecclesiastical or
theological limiting it has no lesson for us ?　I
would remark that it is the same sin of " limiting
the Holy One " that keeps us down in daily life.
To cease to limit God is the strongest and best
stimulus to right doing.　We live ill because we
habitually under-estimate our place in the heart

of God ; we sink into a degradation that at last
becomes a hell in itself because we will not take
our place as the sons of God in the daily duties
of life. We limit the Holy One to His judgment
throne somewhere away in heaven, and deny
Him His Fatherhood in our own homes. We
limit Him to Sunday observances and shut Him
out of the little trials and joys of daily life.
We limit Him to great crises, and talk about
" Providence," and deny that the smallest wants
and sorrows and pleasures of the humblest
individual are as much His care as the law of
gravitation. We limit Him by our pessimism,
and discontent, and habitual want of trust, and
puerile superstitions. In short, instead of believing in the Father, we worship an idol of the
mind ; for all limitation of God, whether mechanical or mental, whether in a dogma or an image,
is idolatry.

Again, how astoundingly we limit the Holy
One by our want of faith in intercession for
others, for the sick, the sorrowful, the desolate,
the dying. It sounds like a paradox, I know,
but we actually cramp and fetter and limit the
benevolent purposes of the All Father because in
our hearts we do not believe that He will answer
our petitions.

It is impossible for me to reduce it to a proposition, though I have seen it, amongst those
who believe in this power of intercession, work
what might be called miracles. The Soul of

Souls, The Supreme Father Spirit, is the inmost
element within us all. When some common interest deeply moves us, when we are all eagerly
desiring the same thing, when we are "in the
Spirit on the Lord's Day," this vital power of the
soul seems to be unlocked. What is it ?   It is
the breath and will of the Infinite. It is not
that it is something from us that acts on God ;
it is something from God that is acting through
us, and the united current of purpose goes forth
as a dynamic force and acts directly upon the
object for which we are praying. When we
doubt, when we will not take our full place in
God, when we withhold mental concentration,
when we ignore the divine nature in us, when
we just languidly make a request and then think
of something else, we hinder this divine outflow
of spiritual sympathy, this wireless current of
God's dynamics ; in other words, we " limit the
Holy One of Israel."

One final application I will make, and I make
it, first, because it is implied in all the Epiphany
gospels, and, secondly, because it answers questions which I hear just now asked upon all sides.
The injunction not to limit the Holy One strikes
at that miserable tendency to religious partisan-
ship which is based upon a jealousy or mistrust
of the spiritual gifts of others who differ from us
in definition. This tendency threatened to break
up the early Church. When in the year 57 St.
Paul wrote to the Corinthians, this mischief,

this poison, was actively at work. Coming events
were casting their shadows before. Some were
saying, " I am of Kephas;" others, " I am of
Paul "; others, " I am of Christ." The " I am of
Kephas" party grew rankly and developed into
the Papacy. The Gospel for the third Sunday
after Epiphany concentrates all the Epiphany
teaching and bruises that serpent's head, by pro-
laiming that the immanence of the Logos is not
the monopoly of Paul, or of Kephas, or even of
those who call themselves by the name of Christ ;
that in every nation, and in every Church, and
in every religion, he that feareth God and worketh
righteousness is accepted with Him ; that many
shall come from the East and from the West :
Japanese from the Far East, trained in the noble
principles of Bushido ; Indian tribes from the
Far West, worshippers of the Great White Spirit ;
they who have lived their lives bravely, purely,
honestly in such light as they possessed, and
shall sit down in the Kingdom, when children of
the Kingdom who have esteemed creed before
life, and orthodoxy before activity, shall be cast
out.

This answers completely the questions which
are being put upon all sides about the remarkable
Welsh Revival and the evangelistic meetings
which are being conducted in the Albert Hall.
" The Welsh Revival," the Churchman asks, " is it
from heaven or of men ? Answer me." It almost
provokes a smile to note the dilemma of the stiff,

unbending Churchman. " If we shall say from
heaven, we shall be acknowledging the active
operation of the Holy Ghost amongst those who
are manifestly schismatics and violent opponents
of our Church. If we shall say of men, we are
wholly at a loss to account for the unmistakable
fruits of the Spirit, love, joy, peace, long-suffering
and the rest." Yes, there is the dilemma. You
cannot explain away these fruits of the Spirit.
If this is transient physical emotion, we can
only say, Thank God for physical emotion. The
reform in the direction of the abounding curse of
intemperance has been truly remarkable in Wales.
On December 31st, the Chief Constable of Cardiff
presented the Mayor with a pair of white gloves,
indicating the absence of a single case brought
before the Court, and this at a time of year
when usually the Court is crowded with cases
of this character. The Bishop of St. David's,
preaching in Pembrokeshire, said that the revival
in Wales had stopped more drunkenness in two
months than Parliament had in two years. Can
physical emotion, neurotic excitement, work
these drastic changes, or is this one more of the
majestic disclosures of the Universal Spirit of
God, who bloweth where He listeth ?

Will it last ? you say. I reply, What does
last ? Did Pentecost last ? Did the whole of
the three thousand there converted hold on to
the end ? Obviously some will backslide, but
many will go on from strength to strength, and

will be faithful unto death. No, you cannot limit the Holy One of Israel. Once predicate intense vitality of Godlike purpose, and quickened spiritual lives will certainly be the result, whether the missioner be a Welsh Dissenter, a Bishop, an American evangelist, a Quaker, or a Cardinal.

But it is asked, What about the meetings in the Albert Hall? Ought Church people to go there? ought they to encourage others to go there? Is not the strict Churchman casting a stigma on his Church by going there? Did not the Bishop of London say that he could take no personal part in services of an undenominational character? This is just a hall for music. It is not a church. Well, you are not under the necessary ecclesiastical limitations which a bishop is, perhaps, bound to recognise. But remember, the promoters of the Albert Hall meetings can claim the noble promise in Ex. xx.: "In all places where I record My Name I will come unto thee, and bless thee." With this promise claimed, every place is a church; without it, no place is a church. The humble dwelling of Aquila and Priscilla, of which we read in the Acts, though probably only a tent, was as much a church as St. Paul's or Westminster Abbey.

But you ask, Will the Name, the real Name, of the Lord be proclaimed there? I believe it will; and if it is not, if the gross and blasphemous libel upon the All Father which is sometimes heard at such meetings be uttered, remember,

men are better than their creeds. And the
world's Father is so habituated to being carica-
tured by definitions, formularies, councils, sects,
"isms," and mistranslations of the Bible, and
yet so yearning for recognition, that even if in
the background of the teaching in the Albert
Hall there does lurk the conventional libel upon
God, the Holy Spirit will still deal with hearts
and lead many to conversion.

No, there is no reason why a Churchman should
not go to the Albert Hall meetings. Do not
condemn any who are casting out demons in
the Master's Name because they walk not with
us. The direction in which the Universal Spirit
is working in our day is against exclusiveness
and towards the freest spiritual communion
amongst those who differ widely as to methods,
creeds, and definitions. When in the Litany we
pray against schism, I personally never consider that I am referring to those who con-
scientiously dissent from the Church of England,
but to the separating elements in our own
community, to the malicious bigotry sometimes
manifested between differing parties in the
Church itself. That is schism if you will. Therefore, as there is one body, namely, all that is ;
and one Spirit, namely, the life of all that is ;
and as this one Spirit is God, and as God is Love,
and as love is endless, and as all men are partakers of the Divine nature, I believe in the
power of human regeneration through the tes-

timony of unordained men whose lips have been
touched by the mystic coal of inspiration from
the altar of the heart of God. I believe in the
new birth, the initiation of the new life, the
kindling of fresh light in souls, through the
Welsh Revival, the meetings in the Albert Hall,
through every form of earnest evangelistic effort.
And if I were to deny it, I should consider that
I was ranking myself with those of whom it
was said of old, " They limited the Holy One of
Israel."

THE AWAKENING.

———

"Awake, thou that sleepest, and arise from the dead, and Christ shall shine upon thee."—*Eph.* v. 14 (R.V.)

ACCEPTING this utterance of the apostle as inbreathed by the Spirit of God, I perceive in this command : First, a suggestion on the universal and spiritual plane ; and, secondly, a practical injunction on the surface plane of common ethics. The spiritual interpretation is luminous with high suggestion, for on this plane the command, Awake ! is the solemn and blessed summons to every departing soul at the moment of that change which we call death. We live in a world of illusion, a condition to which St. Paul tells us we have been exposed, not by our own will, but by the act of God. Here things are not what they seem ; part of our illusion is to call things by their wrong names. We speak of being in the land of the living, whereas human life is only the threshold of the land of the living. We speak of death as falling asleep, whereas it is awakening with a delighted awe to a consciousness of the Universal Parent Spirit impossible to us here. The peace which settles on a dead face is not entirely accounted for by relaxation of the facial muscles. Shelley saw this when he wrote : " Peace, peace, he is not dead, he doth not sleep ; he hath awakened from the dream of life." And I believe that at the moment of death, when you are released from your animal body, those words are somehow spoken, or their sense conveyed, "Awake, thou that sleepest, and arise from the dead, and Christ shall shine upon thee." Wordsworth saw this as well as Shelley. It is said that the only writing of another poet that Wordsworth ever praised, and which he learnt by heart, and of which he used to say, " I wish I had written those lines," were the lines of Mrs. Barbauld :

> Life ! we've been long together
> Through pleasant and through cloudy weather ;
> 'Tis hard to part when friends are dear—
> Perhaps 'twill cost a sigh, a tear ;
> Then steal away, give little warning,
>   Choose thine own time.
>   Say not good-night, but in some brighter clime
> Bid me good-morning.

Yes ; physical death is true life bidding you " good-morning." You have been asleep and dreaming, but now are awake in the glorious morning when the day breaks and the shadows flee away. And at that moment the angel messenger, whom we call death, says, "Awake, thou that sleepest, and arise from the dead, and Christ shall shine upon thee."

But obviously this injunction also reiterates

and elucidates the Easter message. There is but one standpoint from which I find myself able to unfold what to me is the truth of God, without which I could neither think the thought nor speak the words, " Our Father which art in heaven." I believe that one Life, one Soul, one Love is immanent in the universe, one perfect Intelligence is in all, through all, and above all. Only our human limitations lead us to draw distinctions between great and small in this universal Divine Immanence. All forms of matter are expressions of the all-producing Spirit. The all-vital generative energy is as truly operative in the wriggling of a microscopic bacillus as in the evolution of a world. The highest expression of this creative energy is, in this planet, man. And Jesus Christ manifests the perfect ideal of this highest expression, to which perfect ideal all His brethren are predestined ultimately to be conformed, not by leaps and bounds, not by imputed righteousness or schemes of salvation, but by separate and individual emancipation from all that hinders true development, by the slow, gradual conquest of the lower limited life, by the evolution of the higher and universal life. This I believe to be the foundation of religion. I know no other foundation than this. " Other foundation can no man lay," says St. Paul, " than that which is laid : which is Jesus Christ." And Jesus Christ in this sense is more than one Being. He is the revealed name for a prolonged

process—a name that links you with the unthinkable past, for " in the beginning was the
Word, and by Him were all things made ; " that
upholds you in the present, for " He is the light
that, coming into the world, lighteth every man,
and by Him all things consist ; " that makes
the future yours, for " as in Adam all die, even
so in Christ shall all be made alive."

Jesus Christ is the unique manifestor for the
purposes of demonstration of that Divine Word
or Reason of the Absolute which is immanent
in all men.   The children of the Word were lost
in the flesh and needed strong help.   " Foras-
much as the children were partakers of flesh and
blood," we read, " He also Himself likewise took
part of the same."   Children we were before we
were clothed upon with mortal flesh ; we were
" in Him before the foundation of the world."

Now, it is this glorious truth that Christ and
humanity are of the same genus, inasmuch as
humanity is the offspring of God, that lends an
undying power to the Easter festival.   The Word
immanent in man, Incarnate in Jesus, implies
that all His experiences are guarantees of ours,
and that we have found in Him the solution of
the problem of our earthly existence.   And, first,
His undoubted survival after crucifixion and
death has placed the seal of certainty upon the
universal instinct of survival in man.   This
instinct, this hope, this conception that human
life on this earth is but a narrow isthmus be-

tween the two boundless eternities of " whence "
and " whither," has soothed for millions the
harrowing mystery of existence ; this instinctive
moral conviction that " life shall live for ever-
more " has been sealed and certified by the survival of the Christ. That is why Easter is
to us the queen of festivals. His appearances
during the forty days have converted these
presentiments into radiant certainties. St. Paul,
who in his vision on the road to Damascus had
seen the Christ, does not appeal to instinct
or presentiment. He says, " We know that
we have a spiritual body." He knew it, not
because it was whispered in his soul by instinct,
or suggested to his mind by the sap rising in
the tree, or the butterfly emerging from the
chrysalis ; he possessed the evidence that placed
the doctrine of survival upon the basis of
certainty, for Jesus is the representative of the
race, the first-born amongst many brethren, the
perfect specimen of the destiny of humanity.
" As He is, so are we in this world." And
through the organic unity of the body of
humanity the survival of the whole race is
absolutely guaranteed through the manifested
survival of the one perfect member of the
human family.

There are two words which in this context I
would emphasize ; the one is the word " survival," the other is the word " guaranteed."
And first, survival. Why do I emphasize the

word survival ? Because it is the best translation of the Greek word anastasis ; because it is
the word that definitely implies the Christian
revelation that there is no death ; because there
is a tendency in certain quarters to base the
argument for human immortality upon the
resuscitation and reconstruction of the physical
body, and to identify the absolute truth of
the religion of Jesus Christ with the conception
of the reanimation and rising up of His actual
flesh body. This unphilosophic and materialistic
conception has been elaborated in a brilliant
work of fiction called " When it was Dark," a
work which must have been very widely read,
as it is now in its thirty-seventh thousand. The
plot of the story is a conspiracy engineered by
a Jew millionaire who desires to destroy Christianity, and who, with the assistance of heavily
bribed experts, first forges and then professes to
discover near the Damascus Gate at Jerusalem
a stone slab covering a tomb in which is a
mouldering body, and containing the following
inscription in uncial Greek letters : " I, Joseph
of Arimathæa, took the body of Jesus the
Nazarene from the tomb where it was first laid
and hid it in this place." The book goes on to
describe in thrilling detail how the whole fabric
of Christianity was shattered to pieces by this
discovery, and how indescribable darkness and
demoralisation overwhelmed the Christian world.
The Bishop of London alluded to the book in

the following terms : " I wonder whether any
of you have read that remarkable work of fiction,
entitled ' When it was Dark '? It paints in
wonderful colours what it seems to me the world
would be if for six months the Resurrection
might be supposed never to have occurred."

I agree that this work of fiction is remarkable,
but I draw from it a somewhat different inference. To me it paints in lurid colours the
unwisdom of confusing the manifest survival of
the imperishable individuality of the Lord Jesus
with the reanimation of the Hebrew form of flesh
and blood in which, for our sakes, He placed
Himself under limitations. It illustrates the
danger of making the whole Christian faith depend on the identification of the natural body
which was laid to rest in the tomb of Joseph of
Arimathæa with the spiritual body, the astral
body, the materialization in which the Lord
Jesus during forty days manifested to His
disciples the certainty of the continuity of His
individuality. When and from what did the
Lord Jesus rise ? Surely the moment of His
actual rising was the precise moment when He
" cried with a loud voice and gave up the
ghost." Surely He rose out of the body that
He left hanging on the cross, taking with Him
into the intermediate Eden of Paradise the
malefactor who had appealed to Him ; and
passing on Himself with healing in His wings
to the disciplinary department of Paradise

called Hades, probably taking with Him the
other malefactor, and there He " preached to
the spirits in safe keeping who had sinned in
the days of Noah." And on the third day " He
showed Himself alive by many infallible proofs,"
of which showing Easter is the annual com-
memoration. And this divine and immutable
truth would not be affected in the slightest
degree if the forgery imagined in this clever
book were a reality, and if, as Matthew Arnold
says, " the Syrian stars still looked down upon
the body born of Mary." Therefore I emphasize
the word survival.

To me resurrection is not the long-deferred
reconstruction of decayed corpses, but the emancipation of the real individual from flesh surroundings at the moment of death. I recognize
no other resurrection than the resurrection from
the dead, from the dead body. There is no point
in which the division between the Latin and
the Greek conception is more marked. Both
conceptions are enshrined in our formularies.
For example, in the Apostle's Creed, the expression is " Resurrection of the body," and in the
Baptismal Service " Resurrection of the flesh."
Both of these are founded on the Latin conception, which was derived from the Egyptian
religion. In the Nicene Creed, which embodies
the thought of Athanasius, who was the exponent of the teaching of the early Greek fathers,
the expression is, " I look for the resurrection of

the dead." And the phrase used by our Lord is " Resurrection from the dead." And He goes on clearly to show that by " resurrection from the dead " He meant the rising of the immortal part from the dead body. For He says : " But that the dead are raised even Moses showed in the place concerning the bush, when he called the Lord, The God of Abraham, and the God of Isaac, and the God of Jacob. Now, He is not the God of the dead, but of the living ; for all live unto Him," clearly implying that Abraham, Isaac, and Jacob were risen as much and as fully as they ever would rise.

And the next word that I would emphasize is the word " guaranteed," as it tends to wipe away tears from mourners' eyes. Virtually, the non-finality of death is an irresistible inference from every deep and true conception of the Supreme Being. God is the inmost substance in every man, therefore man is immortal, not on account of any attainment, but because the immortality of God is embedded in his nature. We live because God lives. Jesus, the perfect specimen of humanity, projected Himself into visibility after His death, in the presence of chosen witnesses, to demonstrate the identity of His individuality ; and He told us to draw the inference. He said, " Because I live, ye shall live also." We are, therefore, absolutely certain that the life of which we are conscious now is not

3

running out into annihilation, but into development. We are equally absolutely certain that
the loved human friends who have passed from
our sight are alive, conscious, progressing,
evolving. The silver cord of physical life is
loosed, the golden bowl of visible embodiment
is broken, with the result that they are in more
spiritual conditions, in fuller, freer, completer
life. It is altogether irrelevant to ask where
they are. The creaturely accommodation of what
we call locality is probably not an attribute of
that other, as yet unrealizable, sphere of being.
It is clear that there is a mode of existence, a
sphere of being, an unseen universe into which
the individuality of the human being passes
when emancipated from the limitations of the
body. That it is not demonstrable to the senses
is no argument against it. There are multitudes
of sights and sounds in the seen universe which
are not cognizable by the ordinary organs of
sensation and perception. If our natural senses
were at this moment miraculously quickened,
we should find that we were surrounded by
sphere upon sphere of natural activities now
utterly beyond our perceptions. We should
analyze the infinite ether, watch electro magnetic
radiation, listen to the busy weaving of the
microscopic germ-cells that build the substance
of a flower and repair the waste of a human
body, recognize the chemical combinations that
produce the illumination glowing in our electric

lights. These are realities, but they are super-sensuous realities. It is no greater wonder that we should be surrounded by a world which is above, beyond, and around the world of sense. The day will come for all in which our inner faculties will be opened, and we shall see. We were physically alive for some months before we had any evidence of the existence of this world. The day came when the senses which were then in germ opened, and we were face to face with the world. It will be so one day with the unseen world. Then it will not be that anything will appear, but we shall see what is. It is not desirable that these inner eyes shall be opened during the process of human education. Very few are fit for it ; and of those that are fit for it, very few could endure it. Isaiah, Daniel, John were overpowered by it. Some, like Elisha, St. Paul, Swedenborg, Jacob Boehme, John Wesley, have seen into the spirit world and have contributed evidence, from interior sight, of this more exalted plane of human life ; but it is undesirable for the average man.

To live here in that condition of supernatural ecstasy which lays open the secrets of the higher sphere of being would be to live not as men, but as semi-paralysed, wingless angels, useless in this world and not attuned to the other. The appearances of the Risen Christ during the forty days provide for us glimpses of this invisible world surrounding us, which add to the dignity,

the grandeur, the security of this earth life by
assuring us of the close proximity of spiritual
intelligences empowered to act on humanity ;
guiding, arranging, inspiring, protecting. Obviously Christ materialized Himself into the form
or accommodation which would most assure His
doubting followers of the reality of His survival ;
hence upon one occasion the appearance of
wounds, which, of course, afford no analogy of
the spiritual body. If the power of open spiritual
vision were vouchsafed to us, the appearance
would probably be wholly different, as it was to
John at Patmos. Whatever spiritual intelligence
was manifested would assume the shape that
would most assure us of identity. The fact is
the same, the truth is the same. The spiritual
beings in the other world, the human beings who
have passed gloriously into the higher sphere,
are not far away from us or indifferent to us,
but actively, intelligently, influentially occupied
in advancing, by invisible agency, the moral
restitution of mankind. Is it not obvious that
they would do so ? We are surrounded, says
St. Paul, by "an innumerable cloud of witnesses." Amongst them are some of our closest
and dearest : the mother who bore us, the father
who taught us by his forbearing love what the
love of God must be, the child who has gone
before us. Would they not cheer, encourage,
console, protect us, if they could ? And what
are they now ? Individually the same beings,

emancipated from bodily limitations, pulsing in the higher world, " always beholding the face of our Father in heaven "; they are ministering spirits capable of ministering in ways we know not of to those whom on earth they have loved.

Consider for a moment the personal application of the injunction, " Awake, thou." Liberate thought from the material plane. Easter enthusiasm is too apt to centre round the consideration of an historical fact and to evaporate in church decoration and choral alleluias. Historical facts are only manifestations in time relations of eternal truths. Christ, the peculiar embodiment of the all-inclusive Spirit, has abolished death by proving that it is only a change of condition. But Christ is the sacrament, the symbol, of the one infinite life which throbs in every blade of grass, uplifts every seed, and elevates every man. Therefore He is, as He declared, " the resurrection and the life." As Matthew Arnold said : " Despite the failure, sin, and God-defiance still poisoning this fair earth, Christ is risen, in the sense that His cause is conquering. Creeds may be discredited, ancient forms of religion may be in danger, historic Churches may pass away, the old order change and give place to new in all departments of social and political life ; but, nevertheless, the Prince of this world is judged, the victory of Jesus is practically won, the world can never be again what it was before the first Easter Day ; the secret of Jesus

is working as a leaven in humanity, never to
cease working until, either here or hereafter, the
whole is leavened."

There follows the personal question, Is the
secret of Jesus working in me, or am I still
dreaming my life away in the stupor and insen-
sibility of sleep ? What are God's unveilings
worth if they do not mightily influence individual
men ? Resurrection is the breaking into manifestation of a new life within the old life : the
life that thinks high and aims high ; the life
that recognizes the Divine secret within and
deliberately elects to live to develop it in itself
and in others. That is the resurrection life.

Therefore Easter pleads with us to uplift, re-
dedicate, purify our hearts by ennobling our
ambitions, strengthening our resolves, deepening
our aspirations, intensifying our conflict with
evil within and without. The appeal is personal,
individual. Awake, thou, and Christ shall shine
upon thee. Glorious analogy. It is not a matter
of choice or effort for that indefinable, diffusive,
penetrating energy that we call light to shine on
and illuminate all things. Though there is a
volition that can keep us from the light, the sun
does not begin to shine when we open our eyes.
Not otherwise is it with the " light that lighteth
every man coming into the world." Believe it.
The Presence is in thee and all around thee.
Power, wisdom, goodness, love, mercy, these are
the prismatic colours which compose the white ray

of the Presence, bathing in its splendour the spirits
of men.   Awake, thou that sleepest.   Shake off
the moral deterioration of the conscious choice of a
lower standard, and Christ shall shine upon thee.
He cannot help it.   He is shining now, but thou
knowest it not.   It is of the risen Christ, the
ever-present friend of humanity, nearer to each
one of us than He ever was to friend or disciple
on earth, that the truly-inspired lines refer :

> I looked to Jesus, and I found
>   In Him my Star, my Sun ;
> And in that light of life I'll walk
>   Till travelling days are done.

THE MOTHERHOOD IN GOD;
THE MARRIAGE OF THE SOUL;
THE WEDDING GARMENT OF THE SOUL.

"The kingdom of heaven is like unto a certain king who made a marriage for his son."—*Matt*. xxii. 1.

THE esoteric teaching of this Parable is suggestive rather than dogmatic. It appeals not on its surface, but in its inwardness, to the spiritual eye—the intuitive faculty. It veils under a metaphor, and in veiling suggests, a revelation of the immeasurable perfections and inscrutable characteristics of the Infinite Originator called God, and of the mysterious operations of the Creative Will in calling into existence all that is. If we undertake a reverent thought-excursion into this Parable, it is important to bear in mind that, after the custom of the Oriental allegory, the metaphor changes more than once in the course of the narrative. The first suggestion presents itself rather as a preface to the Parable. The human mind, when dwelling seriously and reverently upon the mystery of origins, is apt to ask itself the question, How did the Omnipotent Generative Love, the

Creative Will, produce its child humanity ? The " mechanical engineer " theory of the Creationists being repudiated, how did the eternal idea of a human race pass into realization ? How did the generative thought become transmuted into human beings ? There is, of course, but one answer. We admit at once we do not know ; but that is the attitude of the acquisition of knowledge ; blessed are the consciously ignorant, for theirs is the Kingdom of Knowledge, and the mind liberated from the material plane tentatively follows the gleam as the Kingdom of Knowledge sheds its beams upon the intuitions of humble learners. Jesus quieted much heart restlessness by teaching us to call the Infinite Originator by the familiar name of Father : " Our Father which art in heaven." There is, however, a certain element of incompleteness, of solitariness about the name Father, intimate as it is. If we are the sons of God, who is our mother ? And the heart of man humbly wonders whether it would be justified in conceiving, even without expressing, a tenderer, a more intimate name for God, even than the name Father. Is it just possible that we are falling into the error of a limitation of which the Eastern thinkers were never guilty in designating the Infinite Originator by the masculine pronoun alone ?

In thinking out this problem, we turn naturally to that suggestive pastoral Idyll of the Garden of Eden, in the beginning of Genesis ; that fascinating compound of legend, allegory, and revelation which exists in some form in the early legends of all religions. It is there stated that God created man " after His own image," or, perhaps, should it be after *their* own image, for the words are " let *us* make man in our image "; and the narrative affirms that He made man male and female, and called their name Adam (the well-known difficulty of the fusing of the two accounts in Genesis, the Eloistic the earlier, and the Jahvistic the later, does not seem to affect this point).

It is clear, then, that this first son of God called Adam, whether a race or an individual does not here signify, was, before the separation of woman, bisexual ; that is, he combined in unity the perfections of male and female, and it was as male and female in unity that Adam was in the likeness of God. This affirmation of the bisexuality of the first man as a mirror of his Maker involves an inference of profound beauty and consolation. The " Father " conception of God is a noble advance upon the older Deism, but to be justified in predicating motherhood also of the Infinite Spirit is to introduce a closer, tenderer, more appealing relationship. The recognition of this thought is traceable throughout Scripture from the very first. The Hebrew word for the Spirit of God which moved upon the waters is a feminine word ; the word translated " moved " signifies " brooded," as

the mother bird broods over her young. The
Hebrew word for Father is feminine in the plural,
and we learn from the Kabbala that the plural
word Elohim, when used in the singular, is
feminine. The suggestion is ever emerging from
the more tender passages which are occasionally
discoverable in the Old Testament : " As one
whom his mother comforteth, so will I comfort
you " ; " Can a woman forget her sucking child
. . . yet will I not forget thee "; and in the self-
revelation of God in the Incarnation, the Divine
motherhood is suggested in the saying, " Even
as a hen gathereth her chickens under her
wings." Blessed is the thought that motherhood is enfolded in the nature of the Absolute ;
it is a contemplation calculated to fill the heart
with a new and more tranquil and more perfect
rest in the Lord.

At first, apparently, this bisexual being or
race called Adam was commanded to be fruitful
and multiply after the manner in which the
Creative Spirit in whose image he was made
was fruitful and multiplied ; and there, of course,
we are at once out of our depth. It is mere
presumption to attempt to fathom the method
of the origin of the life of evolution in the
universe ; perhaps we shall know when sex-dis-
tinction passes into some higher, nobler state of
perfected humanity, in a more spiritual sphere
than this. Meanwhile, it is sufficient to draw
the inference that there is as much Motherhood

in God as Fatherhood, and the inference satisfies many yearnings. A cultivated Brahmin once said to me, " I would use daily your Paternoster if I might say, Our Mother which art in heaven." I replied that, in my opinion, the self revelation of God fully justified his paraphrase.

After this mystical suggestion, there comes a change in the allegorical history of origins in Genesis : the woman is separated from the man. There is nothing in the Hebrew about a rib, it is just dichotomy, severing in half. Whether this severance of the bisexual nature was effected on the physical or the psychical plane I know not, but the woman became a separate being, the other half of man. " Bone of my bone," said Adam, " flesh of my flesh, therefore shall she be called Isha," or, as in the East, Ayesha, " because she was taken out of Ish." I do not ask why. I agree with Luther that when once your trust in God is adequate, you have no further use for the question why. But I see that man is about to pass, at that period of his history, from the non-moral condition of innocence to the moral condition consequent upon the knowledge of good and evil. He is to learn self-knowledge, self-control, regulation of natural appetites, that he may become a moral being, through the experience of the possibility of the immoral ; that he may recognize virtue by the experience of being confronted with its opposite. I will follow this thought no further ; it would

be inexpedient ; but some will understand me
when I say that to me the Phallic interpretation
of the Eden story, and the tree in the midst of
the garden, is the true interpretation ; and as
nothing can conceivably occur that has not
been pre-determined by God, Augustine's exclamation as to the so-called " fall," "*O felix
culpa*," O happy fault, O blessed transgression,
was true in a wider sense than he probably
intended when he used the words.

In the meantime, marriage is the foreshadowing
of the time when division of sex shall be no
more, when there will be no longer male and
female, but all one in Christ Jesus. And the
sacramental, creative, inter-blending of the sexes
becomes the favourite metaphor in Holy Scripture of the fruit-bearing union between the
universal Creative Spirit of God and the differentiated entity of the individual spirit of man,
and this thought is the foundation stone upon
which this Parable stands. Starting from the
axiom that humanity is the Incarnation and
Jesus the perfect Archetypal specimen of
humanity, and therefore transcendently divine,
then Jesus is sonship *in excelsis*—spiritual virility
in perfection. He seeks to blend His glorious
life with the potential dormant receptive germ of
the same life in all, that He may impregnate
it with fresh vitality and cause it to be fertile.
" In this," He said, " is My Father glorified,
that ye bear much fruit "; but He also said,

"Apart from Me ye can do nothing." In our Lord's preface to His marriage Parable He says, " The kingdom of heaven is like a certain king who made a marriage for his son." In this suggestive Parable the Absolute is the " certain King " who made a marriage for His Son, and the marriage is between the Logos Incarnate in Jesus and the Logos immanent in the race. He would unite the Perfect Son with the potential sonship in each of the brethren of the race. So Jesus is the appeal of God to the human spirit. God, in presenting to us the Incarnation, points us to Jesus as He did through the voice on the Mount of Transfiguration. He says, *Ecce Homo*, Behold the Man ; potential Divine germ in each separate human being, I appeal to thee, I ask thee, " Wilt thou have this Man to thy wedded Husband ; wilt thou obey Him and serve Him, and keep thee only unto Him ? " And where the awakening Divine germ of sonship in man answers with keen enthusiastic purposeful intent " I will," " Whom have I in heaven but Thee, and who is there on earth that I desire in comparison with Thee ? " " I need Thee, precious Jesu," " Jesus, my Shepherd, Husband, Friend," do you imagine that He will ever let thee go ? Not till heaven, not till earth pass away.

Remember, this is not my metaphor, it is God's metaphor. " Thy Maker is thy husband," He says ; " I am My beloved's and He is mine."

The Scripture simply overflows with the analogy, and it indicates a close binding sacramental fertile union between the soul and God. Obviously there are obligations and requirements on the part of the human soul thus united to the Christ, such as self-surrender, obedience, fidelity. In James iv. 4, where the words "adulterer and adulteress" are used, the true translation, insisted on by the American revision committee, is, "Ye who break your marriage vow to God." But He will never break His vow to us. "Those whom God" in His eternal purpose before the world was "hath thus joined together" let no man imagine that he can ever finally put asunder.

Now at this point the metaphor, as is so often the case in our Lord's allegories, changes completely. The profound mystic thought of the human soul as the Bride of Christ passes, and our attention is directed to the wedding guests and the wedding garment, and the change in the metaphor introduces the personal application of the Parable. Responsibility for discernment of moral condition belongs to the guest alone; power of discernment belongs to the King alone. A well-known Oriental custom is laid under contribution for the imagery of the Parable : the King has provided a wedding garment ; it is prepared for every guest of whatever condition ; each guest has the sole responsibility for being clothed in it ; it is manifestly something spiritual, ethereal, immaterial, invisible, for there is no suggestion that a fellow guest or a servant of the King can perceive its absence in another ; only the King's eye can perceive this, for " the Lord seeth not as man seeth, for man looketh upon the outward appearance, but the Lord looketh upon the heart." The King comes in and perceives one (one here, as so often in Scripture, being the type of a class) who is not clothed with the garment. To " stand before God " is judgment ; no need for words, it is to see things as they are, with all false standards gone, and to be self-condemned.

The unclothed must go forth for a while into educative darkness ; he has nothing in common with that community ; there is no such thing as going to heaven without affinity for heavenly things. His title was clear enough, the King had sent for him ; his meetness was lacking. The universality of Divine Sonship is a fact ; its in-dividual application is contingent on co-operation. The redeemed are all men ; the saved are those that know it, and to know it is not to talk it, or even to ape its actions, but to be it.

What is the garment, the absence of which is perceptible to the King alone ? We are told that it is the righteousness of Christ. It is true ; but a misapprehension of the phrase is responsible for a perverted Gospel. It is incon-ceivable, nay, it would be immoral if it were some gorgeous external covering for our self-

made rags of hypocrisy, or lust, or pride ; if it
were a quality imputed to us while we remained
the same as we were before. Such expressions as
" imputed righteousness," " imputed merits of
Christ," are not Scripture ; Scripture speaks of
being presented holy and without blemish ; holy
by a righteousness imparted, not imputed. George
Fox, the founder of the Society of Friends, said,
" The righteousness of Christ is the spiritual
man's own livery." How did St. Paul define the
wedding garment ? " Put off," he says, " the
old man which is corrupt, according to the deceitful lusts, and be renewed in the spirit of your
minds ; and put on the new man, which after
God is created in righteousness and true holiness."
The wedding garment, then, is not assumed
from without, it is evolved from within ; its germ
is implanted in all men, in man's inmost spiritual
self ; it is the Kingdom of Heaven within ; it
must be born (the Greek word is ἄνωθεν) " from
above," from Heaven, from the Heaven within,
quickened into life by the Heaven above, fed
and nourished by the Heaven around, which is
the Divine humanity of Jesus, accessible in
prayer, sacrament, and meditation, and by
whose presence the life is enfolded. Watch the
peacock butterfly spreading his gorgeous wings
to the sun. Whence came that resplendent
wedding garment ? The King gave it him, ἄνωθεν
from above, from within ; He did not impute it,
but impart it. But the butterfly was not always

4

thus ; the germ of the jewelled robe lay hid in
the dingy caterpillar that once he was ; he
evolved it himself by simple obedience to the
law of his life. All the caterpillar nature slowly
ministering to the butterfly nature, he lived it
out, and it automatically clothed upon him. If
you could imagine a caterpillar taking its place
amongst butterflies with its gem-like robe unevolved, you have a Parable of a child of God
in the presence of the King with his new man,
his spiritual self unevolved, and his old man
with its carnal desires and deceitful lusts mono-
polizing him. The clothing of the new man is
our character ; we are weaving the robe with
our own hands day by day ; it reveals itself to
us by the bent and inclination of our lives.
Before the Majesty of God we stand to-day.
He, as He comes amongst us gathered in His
temple, perceives whether purity is whiter,
gentleness increasing, submission more real, helpfulness more habitual, prayer more constant,
temper more controlled, life more Christ-like.
I cannot judge you, you cannot judge me, no
fellow guest can see the wedding garment ; the
King judges us both. Is He saying now, here
to-day, to me—to you—

FRIEND, HOW CAMEST THOU IN HITHER NOT
HAVING ON A WEDDING GARMENT ?

THE ORIGIN OF MAN.

"Hereby perceive we the love of God, because He laid down His life for us."—1 *John* iii. 16.

And the 24th verse :—

"And hereby we know that He abideth in us, by the Spirit which He hath given us."

THOUGHTFUL questions have reached me in connection with the previous sermon, in which I affirmed that there is at least as much Motherhood as Fatherhood in God, and that the Brahmin was justified in his desire to paraphrase the Paternoster in the words, "Our Mother which art in heaven." I am asked how the human race was generated under this profound conception of bi-sexuality in the Infinite Originating Spirit, of which bi-sexuality Adam, before the separation of woman, was an image and a type. In what sense can we understand the Scripture genealogy of the race, "Which was the son of Adam, which was the son of God?"

I repeat what I then said : we do not know, we cannot know. Professor Max Müller said that we must divest the words Father and Son of their customary significance if we would touch even the fringe of the profound relation between

God and man. But this utterance of St. John suggests thought, for it hints that man's origin was through some mystical process of "laying down," distributing, diffusing God's unthinkable and marvellous creative life, the image and type of which is the human father diffusing his life, and the human mother giving of her very life when a child is born into the world.

"Hereby perceive we the love of God, because He laid down His life for us." I contend that this mystic utterance is obviously not exhausted by its surface interpretation, which may fairly be considered as referring to the voluntary self-sacrifice upon the cross of the one Perfect Representative of the human race ; not exhausted, I say, because Calvary is a manifestation in time relations of an Eternal truth, and of a perpetual attitude of the Infinite Spirit who embodied His moral nature for purposes of recognition in the Man Christ Jesus.

To grasp the depth, the fulness, the comprehensiveness of this utterance the power of thought must reach beyond the manifestation of love on the Cross of Calvary. It is when we have thought ourselves to height beyond limitation, and beyond Deism, that we are in a position to interpret the expression, "He laid down His life for us." Who is the "He" who laid down His life for us ? And how did He lay down His life ? You say, obviously, Jesus, He laid down His life for us. Yes, because Jesus is God under a limitation; but here thought may travel beyond this blessed world-saving embodiment of the fulness of God under the limitation called Jesus. The one personal pronoun in the universe is God. The Authorised Version has inserted the word "God," the translators obviously inferring that the Greek word ἐκεῖνος, "that one," could refer only to the Supreme Creative Intelligence. It is, then, God who laid down His life for us. The Supreme Cause of causes, the Infinite Originator, "laid down His life," and He laid it down "for us." Obviously, then, the expression "laid down His life" cannot, in that sphere of interpretation, refer to what we commonly understand by "dying." To speak of dying in connection with the self-existent One is an absurd contradiction in terms. I think the secret of the expression is discoverable in the following axioms, which the laws of clear philosophic thought demand, namely : (1) the universal responsible Fatherhood of the Unconditioned Intelligence that men call God, and (2) that one life, one love, one intelligence pulses through all that is. Granting these axioms, certain corollaries follow. God "laying down His life," the Unconditioned Intelligence laying down His life, and laying it down for us, would obviously refer to His laying it down in what is commonly called Creation, but which I prefer to call Divine Generation. God, under the constraint of love, laying down, diffusing, differentiating His un-

thinkable being, His all-producing Spirit into the
limitations of what we call matter ; the Creator
evolving the creaturely form in the natural
creation, wherein He is hidden, till that form
comes to due self-consciousness and self-assertion ;
God thus becoming the all-containing Soul, Life,
Love, in all that is; and having thus " laid
down His life " in nature, He realises Himself
in man as the highest expression of His diffused
" laid down " life on this planet.

Is it difficult to think this thought ? It may
be, because all real thought is an effort ; but it
is not so great a strain on the thinking capacity
as the attempt made by materialists to free the
universe from an originating mind ; or the
"mechanical engineer" conception of the Creationists, who talk about God making worlds
out of nothing ; or the conventional Dualism
which virtually accounts for the facts of the
world by attributing them to two supreme
powers, one good and the other bad. " He laid
down His life for us," by the transmutation of
thought into matter, that we might be, and He
did it under what Emerson calls the "beautiful
necessity" of producing a race worthy of being
loved and capable of loving. He, God, the unthinkable Cause of Causes, laid down, distributed
His life in humanity. This I have always considered to be the hidden meaning of the parable
of the prodigal son. In that parable the Father
divided unto the younger son, humanity, His life

($\beta\iota o\varsigma$) that He might receive him back, after education, into the Eternal home.

The thoughts that flow from this interpretation are almost bewildering in their blessedness, and in the dignity they imply for humanity. There follows from it the indestructible divinity in man. God laid down, divided, unto humanity, His life. Then the essence of God, the vitality of God, is rooted in man's inmost self, " in Him we live and move and have our being "; and the reverse of the proposition is true, in us He lives and moves and has His being. We are personal spirits who have proceeded from God to matter. Our very inmost being is a portion of God's own essence. The life which the Absolute " laid down " for each one of us when we came by human birth into this sphere of education is ultimately irresistible ; it will work in us, must work in us, until at last we represent in our character and conduct the fulness and unity of God. There is unspeakable rest, amidst the perplexing problems of this world, in the conviction that our individual lives and the lives of those most dear to us are expressions of this universal life that was " laid down," distributed. God's life in man is man's absolute guarantee of final salvation ; we and the Infinite Spirit are one. We do not yet know it as a fact of conscious experience ; the One perfect Specimen of the race did know it as a conscious experience. He knew that He was a perfect expression of the

Universal Soul, of which at present we are imperfect expressions. He could say, "He that hath seen Me, hath seen the Father-Soul," "the Father in Me doeth the works," "I and the Father are one"; but His perfection is the prophecy and guarantee of ours, for Jesus and humanity are the same genus. He spoke of the Absolute as "My Father and your Father." He claimed for us that we are brethren and co-heirs. We have the same origin, the same nature, the same future; and this truth brilliantly illuminates the expression, "Hereby perceive we the love of God, because He laid down His life for us" in order that we might be. That is the only answer I can give to the questions put to me.

Now, the 24th verse, which I have also quoted, comes as a corollary to this profound thought, as indicating (1) that this "laid down" Divine life will always abide in us; and (2) that there are symptoms by which we can know a little of this truth of God's "laid down" life in the soul of man. "Hereby we know that He abideth in us, by the Spirit which He hath given us."

"He abideth in us"—that first; that is an elemental fact to which no contradiction is possible. His "laying down," differentiating, His life in man is not a transitory, experimental flash of divine complacency to be repented of and withdrawn: He abides. Then, secondly, we ought to know it, for there are indicated certain

occasional rich human experiences which are to
be taken as evidences of this abiding. " Hereby
we know that He abides, by the Spirit that He
has given us." Now, that is the inwardness of
the whole of the Epiphany teaching, the abiding
immanence of God, Epiphanised in Jesus, potential in all men. St. John says He abides, and he
implies that we ought to know it. We ought to
know it, though it is true whether we know it
or not.

Does not this put before us a philosophy of
life that lifts us many atmospheres above the
narrow limitations of rudimentary conceptions ?
Does it not affirm (1) the irrevocability of the
Divine immanence, (2) the universality of human
sonship, (3) the blame which attaches to believers
in the Christian revelation if they fail to recognise the abiding of God ?

(1) Consider the glorious confidence that should
be inspired by the assurance that He abides in
us.

Can His infinite purpose, then, be ever rendered ultimately futile and abortive by the self-
conscious, self-determining obstinacy of my finite
mind ? God's purpose, immanent in human
nature, must prove ultimately stronger than all
human perversion. Based upon the proposition
" He abides," " the haunting oracles that stir
our clay " have lost their power. " If I go down
into hell Thou art there." Nay, Thou goest
down with me, for Thou abidest in me. What

care I, then, for the unanswerable problem of
the mystery of evil except to recognise it as a
constant challenge to do good ? If He abides
in humanity, the whole mystery of evil and all
its terrifying cross-working purposes must be
completely under the Divine over-rule, because
it is He, abiding in man, who is confronted by
these resisting agencies. As God lives and moves
and has His being in creation, there can be no
omnipotent or everlasting rival to the one Author
and Indweller of the Universe. There can be no
rival at all except as a divinely-provided resisting
agency, which is a stimulus to progress.

Again, why should I care for speculations
about Biogenesis or Heterogenesis and all the
rest ? In the course of last year certain experiments were conducted which seemed to revive
once more the theory of spontaneous generation.
More than once I was asked with anxiety what
I thought would be the result upon men's faith
if it were proved that spontaneous generation
had really been affected at last in the chemical
laboratory. A painstaking and perfectly honest
investigator imagined that by the effect of radium
upon sterilised bouillon he had produced protoplasm, and the Creationists cry aloud, If this is
true, God is dead. Well, the Creationists' conception of God died some time ago. Alfred
Russell Wallace and Charles Darwin were the
executioners. But suppose this scientist's bouillon was really sterilised (which is very doubtful),

and suppose he had really produced protoplasm, what then ? Who knows anything about protoplasm ? In a body recently dead there is protoplasm, and still warm, but there is no life. But, for the sake of argument, grant that protoplasm is the first medium of life known to us, what then ? Oh, say the timid ones, if the passage from the inorganic to the organic has taken place in the laboratory, a death blow has been inflicted on the supernatural. I answer, they who stand on the glorious words, "God laid down His life" and God "abideth in us," have long ago erased the word "supernatural" from their vocabulary. There is nothing more supernatural than nature. Nature is one of the expressions of the "laid down" life of God ; therefore it is not possible to conceive of anything being super or above nature. There is One Life laid down in the universe. There may be, there is, infinite variety of expression of this one life ; it may be different in the mineral, the crystal, the protoplasm, the amœba, in radium, and in sterilized bouillon, but the only "ousia," substance, in the universe is the Spirit of God which abides. You may have produced protoplasm in your laboratory by the action of radium upon sterilized bouillon ; I doubt it. But if you have, you have illustrated that one of the multitudinous expressions of the immanent self-evolving Spirit that abides is radium acting on sterilized bouillon, and that is all you have proved.

(2) Think, again, how this utterance proves the universality of human sonship, and knocks the bottom out of that irrational contempt for men of another colour, and that miserable spirit of denominational exclusiveness which makes standing with God depend on correctness of definition. "By the Spirit which He hath given us." Who are included in "us"? Only they who have heard and accepted the Christian revelation of the Absolute? Is that so? How can it be, when St. Paul says that this truth of the Logos in man, the "Spirit which He hath given us," was a fact from the foundation of the world, and was revealed, not initiated, by the Incarnation. The Christ revealed and manifested the eternal truth that God had given His Spirit to man, but this eternal truth is "from the foundation of the world," and is the monopoly of no age, no race, no Church, no religion. It is the common spiritual force which has striven for expression in all the great historic religions of the world. We have had our attention lately strongly drawn to the Japanese. To what do you ascribe the mind of that nation as a whole? whence arise the quiet self-reliance of the people through the war, the patient endurance of the bitter anguish of separation from loved ones by death? They are not professing Christians; that is, it is not given to them as yet to acknowledge Jesus as the complete and perfect manifestation of God. Shintoism, Budd-

hism, Confucianism, Laoism, all have had their
share in producing the national spirit.   To the
Japanese death simply does not exist.   History
has no parallel to the solemn and pathetic scene
when Admiral Togo reported to the spirits of
those who had fallen before Port Arthur in the
course of the siege the crowning triumph of the
Japanese arms : " Your corporeal existence has
ceased, but it is my privilege and duty to report
our successes to the spirits of those who sacrificed
their earthly life for the attainment of so great an
end.   May this bring peace and rest to them."
It is the very language of a believer in the communion of saints, and yet they are not professing
Christians.   Are they excluded from the saying,
" The Spirit which He hath given us "?   Surely
they come under the definition of Justin Martyr,
in his first apology, where he says, " Those who
lived according to the Logos " (and the Logos is
the laid down life of God—the Spirit which He
hath given us) " were really Christians, though
they have been thought to be Atheists."   The
Logos, " the Spirit which He hath given us,"
brings hearts to the Father God in different ways,
and, when they get there, it is, in a sense, Jesus
who brought them there, because it was that " laid
down," distributed, life of God, which was specifically Incarnate in Jesus, that brought them
there ; and He who said with perfect knowledge,
" Before Abraham was, I am," and who thus
identified Himself with the Divine Logos from

the foundation of the world, would be fully
justified in saying, even of those who found God
before He " for us men and for our salvation
came down from Heaven," " No man cometh
unto the Father except through Me." *And
surely the lesson of this to Christian believers is
one of breadth, of expansiveness, of realization
of the solidarity of the race, of the universality
of God's " laid down " life ; the lesson of the
duty of discovering, under the rudimentary conceptions of past ages, and the religious instincts
of the so-called heathen races of to-day, the truly
spiritual ideas that they are dimly struggling to
express ; and, if we must evangelize them, as
we must, as the Lord Jesus has bid us do so, to
give back to them, elevated, illuminated, am-
plified, fulfilled, interpreted in Jesus Christ, the
Godward thoughts which have arisen in them
from the Spirit God hath given to humanity.

The final and culminating lesson from this
utterance of St. John is the culpability which
attaches to professing believers in the Christian
revelation for being in ignorance that God
abides in them. St. John implies that we ought
to know that God abideth in us, not only because
He has said so, but by the witness of the Spirit
that He hath given us. The witness of the
Spirit ; that strange, secret whisper of a higher
life, that intuitive protest of the heart against
unregulated animal appetites, that occasional
strong desire of the soul to mount upwards ;

what is that ?   It is God's " laid down " life in
us, it is the energizing of the Divine " Spirit that
He hath given us," bearing witness that God
abideth in us.   We ought to know it, and
knowing it ought profoundly to affect our lives.

Suppose we really lived in the knowledge,
would it be possible solemnly to repeat with
realization the truth, " God abideth in me," and
at the same time deliberately surrender the self
to a mere animal standard ?   No !   If we knew
we were temples of the Holy Ghost, we should
keep the temple pure.   I pray that I and you
may learn the lesson.   I am, you are, one of
those in whom God hath " laid down," expressed,
His life.   We know that He abides in us by the
stirring and the protest of the Spirit He hath
given us.

May we, then, live for eternity, without
pessimism, without uncertainty, without fear.

May we recognize in every trial, in every
disappointment, our Father's promise of the
nobler manhood and womanhood that He is
evolving in us.

May we believe that Jesus is the guarantee
of all this the proof of all this, the specimen of
all this ;   the fulfilment of all aspirations, the
crown and consummation of all religions, the
sacrament of universal life ;   and more even than
this (for He is the same yesterday, to-day, and
for ever), the mighty, wise, ever accessible Friend
of humanity, through whom in all moments of

weakness we have access unto the Father, who abideth in us, through the Spirit which He hath given unto us.*

* The first part of this Sermon has already appeared in print in a previous volume.

WHEAT AND TARES.

"Let both grow together until the harvest."—
Matt. xiii. 30.

THE Parable of the wheat and the tares encourages reverent investigation beyond that rudimentary explanation vouchsafed by our Lord, as adapted to the twilight days of human apprehension. Considered, however, first upon this surface plane of thought, it is important not to misunderstand its application. It is quite clear what it does not mean. It does not provide to God's sons an excuse for standing idle in the midst of God's battle. It does not condemn the labour of reformers who are resisting the development, and eradicating the causes, of moral and physical evil in the world. To suffer the sharp edge of the eternal distinction between right and wrong, good and evil, to be blunted under the excuse that Christ taught us in this Parable to let both grow together till the harvest is to distort Scripture, to sin against humanity, to deny the power of the Gospel ; such an interpretation would have paralyzed the efforts of the Slavery Abolitionists and rendered impossible

5

every great crusade against specific evils that
oppress the race. Poison weeds when recognized
must be eradicated ; against them Christian men
must ever wage daring, ceaseless warfare.

Again, still in the surface plane of interpretation, it is equally clear what this saying does
mean. It is a Divine rebuke against the sense-
less intermeddling of religious controversialists
of every age with their narrow idea of rooting
out of the field of the Church all that does not
seem to them to be orthodox wheat. It is the
clear declaration that the spiritual eye of neither
Bishop, Cardinal, nor Quaker, neither of high,
low, or broad Church, is sufficiently sensitive to
perceive the Divine distinction in religious definition between wheat and tares, and that they
must leave the question of orthodoxy to the
angels. Christendom slips back into Paganism
under the tare-pulling crusades of the sects.
The civil wars of the Churches unchristianize
the morals of the world. Donatus, the Bishop
of Carthage of the fourth century, began this
tare-pulling immorality, and persecuted with fire
and sword all who saw not eye to eye with him,
and it was with this Parable that Augustine con-
founded the theories of Donatus. The spirit of
Donatus has never died. The accursed cruelties
of the Inquisition, the burning and torturing of
Protestants under Mary and Catholics under
Elizabeth, the now happily removed disabilities
of Roman Catholics in Ireland, of Nonconformists

in England, the brutal massacres of Jews in Russia, all are proofs that the surface teaching of this Parable is a constant need of the Church. It is a blessing that the laws of civil liberty in this country are in this matter on the side of the angels.

Let all such tares and wheat grow together indiscriminately till God's harvest. Hold intensely, unflinchingly, your own religious convictions, but keep your fingers off your brother's faith. Bills of excommunication, whether from the Vatican, or from Protestant alliances, or from High Church sacerdotalists, are not only contrary to the spirit of this Parable, but relegated by civilization to the limbo of exploded fallacies. Let him who loves his Church make it lovely by his life and witness. Botanists tell us that the result of sowing darnel or tares among wheat is to stimulate the wheat to abnormal efforts of growth to out-top the darnel. That is the only legitimate Sectarianism, and at the harvest it will not be the Church with the longest pedigree, but the Church with the purest record, that will be gathered as wheat into the garner.

The true power of this Parable, however, lies in its deepest application, and to seek to apply it is no disloyalty to our Lord's surface interpretation; for He Himself told us that His teaching was preparatory, and only calculated for the then standard of reception, and that

His Spirit should take of His words and show them to us. The golden key that the Spirit has put into our hands to unlock this Parable is the expression, " The Kingdom of Heaven is within you."

The whole scene of the Parable in this sense is a deep lesson of the mingled blessedness and awfulness of human life, and it throws an electric beam of light into the dark mystery of evil which hangs like a funeral pall over creation.

The complex being that I call myself is the field, the subject of these two sowings, the Divine and the earthly, the natural and the spiritual, the wheat and the tare. The tare within me (the lower nature) has a high and sacred use, although the sower of it is, for allegorical pur- poses, called " the enemy "—philosophically and inwardly it would be more descriptive to say " the Resister "—that personification who, in the poem of Job, takes his orders from the Almighty ; and the tare has a sacred use, inasmuch as con- tradiction is a condition of moral life. Spiritual growth is an energetic struggle to outlive and outgrow that which contradicts it. The true vigour of the human soul emerges from deep contrasts ; the tare therefore becomes positively a condition of good in this sphere of education.

The power to realize this will depend not a little upon the extent to which we have pene- trated into the secret of that element of an- tagonism which we call moral evil. It seems to me that there is only one working philosophical explanation of the phenomenon called evil, and that it is from that standpoint alone that any man can logically or hopefully struggle against it. When once you have grasped the universality and perfection of God, when, with St. Paul, you can say, " Of Him and through Him and to Him are all things," and have cured yourself of the tendency to make mental exceptions, you will have recognised that any definition short of " God in all and all in God " virtually annihilates the conception of Omnipotence ; you will have taken leave for ever of that miserable materialism which down the ages has referred good and evil to different elemental creative sources ; you will recognize the logical impossibility of any essence, person, matter, spirit, principle, co-existing in antagonism to the resistless omnipotence of God for even the fraction of a second. You believe, without a shadow of mental reservation, that, in all the apparent contradiction and paradox, there is only one principle at work, only one love pulsing, only one purpose evolving, only one end possible, which was involved from the very beginning. You perceive that there cannot be good without an opposite whereby to recognize it ; that the true life of divine sonship can only emerge from deep contrasts ; that contradiction is a condition of all life, physical, moral, spiritual ; that the tare is necessary to the wheat ; that in a sinless, painless world the moral element would be wholly lacking; that, for want of the contrast, goodness in such a world would have no significance in the conscious life of man.

In the pastoral idyll of the Garden of Eden, the allegorical Adam may have been innocent, but he could not be virtuous; he may have been sinless, but he was also characterless. Character comes upon the scene when an alternative is presented between higher and lower; and even, though under the test of this alternative, he failed, the verdict of his Creator was, "he has now become as one of Us"; that is, the Divine is awakened within him because he knows good and evil.

Where the Eternal is represented as saying, " I create evil, saith the Lord," it is perfectly clear that it means that the conscious stirring of His indwelling life creates a standard which causes certain actions and attitudes to be evil by contrast with the standards which were not evil before the standard was given.

I create shadows, saith the sun. There were no shadows till I arose; all was dark together. Now I have arisen, and shadows are because of me.

Evil is unregulated desire. Previous to the existence of the regulation no desire could be evil. I had not known sin, says St. Paul, but for the law. The stirring of the Divine within initiates the regulation, establishes the law written in the heart ; therefore the Divine within alone makes evil possible, and the possibility of evil and the capacity to violate the regulation can alone cause the Divine within to be recognized, to be voluntarily chosen, to be obeyed.

Now if, to this extent, we have penetrated into the secret of evil, one conclusion is clear : the struggle between the wheat and the tare becomes more real, it is taken out of the allegorical into the practical. It is no longer " Michael and his angels fighting the dragon," while Olympus resounds with mystic battle-cries. It is the evolving Divine nature within us convincing us of the wrongness of certain attitudes and actions which, without the Divine nature, would not be wrong. And the one test of the growth of sonship within us will be an instinctive and increasing desire to enlist the whole of our higher faculties against the contrast, the resisting agency that we perceive within us ; and in exact proportion to the extent and activity of our knowledge of the " Christ in us, the hope of glory " will be our estimate of the malignity of moral evil.

" Oh ye that love the Lord, see that ye hate the thing that is evil."

So far, then, as we are concerned as individuals, the sphere of our conflict, the school of our education, the field in which is planted the wheat and the tare, is within. " The Kingdom of Heaven is within." There is the wheat, the

Divine that makes the standard. " Out of the heart proceed adulteries," etc. There are the tares, the human tendencies, that the indwelling divine has caused to be evil; that is Michael and his angels fighting the dragon.

The main lessons, then, that we learn from this interpretation of the Parable are : first, that sinless perfection is, in this age, a dream ; for the tare, the lower nature, will be with us to the end of the age, and the age ends for us when we die. Death is the end of the world to every man. The distressing consciousness of abiding evil tendency even in the truly converted is thus in full accordance with the Divine verdict, " Let both grow together "; while the perpetual counteraction of the lower tendency is the promise to those who abide in Christ. Secondly, it assures convincingly that evil will have an end, that we need not accept as true the faith-shattering doctrine of the perpetuity of moral evil. To believe in two co-eternal principles is fatal to serious belief in the exist- ence of God ; to assert that any other being or person or essence can exist eternally side by side with our Father and eternally resist Him is to dethrone and deny God, and to leave us Atheists in all but name. And lastly, we see clearly the sphere of our individual effort. We are to grow Godwards. The germ of God's wheat within, the Divine nature, is God's inworking ; this is to be met by our forth-putting : " Work out your own salvation, for it is God that worketh in you." We are to believe that the Father has brought us into recognizable relationship with Himself through the manifestation of the Incarnation, that He has an eternal purpose concerning us, is willing His will within us ; and our duty is the work of training, exercising, unfolding, perfecting all our faculties, moral, spiritual, intellectual, in this sense. This will, of course, entail a strong and continuous effort to live to God daily in the little things of life ; live in the Father's presence in small things, in temper, in tongue, in thought, in the humblest occupations, and the great things will take care of themselves.

This is growing ; this is the wheat, the Divine nature, overtopping the tare, and cutting off its supplies. The progress may be gradual, it may be hardly perceptible ; all true growth is slow ; but it is sure, and it is the overcoming life, for it is His life, the life of God revealed in Christ, which we are working out ; and the end of such a life will surely be a glad surprise when God's angel-reapers gather out of the field of our complex humanity all that has darkened and saddened and wearied, and bind them in bundles to burn them, and our true self, our real, indestructible Divine ego, is gathered into His garner.

OUGHT THE CLERGY TO CRITICIZE THE BIBLE?

THE three prominent lessons of the altar Scriptures for the fifth Sunday after Trinity are obvious, comprehensive, and elevating. They are :—

1. The true principle of spiritual discovery : "Launch out into the deep."

2. The secret of the cultivation of the Divine in man : "Sanctify in your hearts Christ as Lord."

3. The sphere in which the lower nature most effectually resists the evolution of this Divine in man : "Let him refrain his tongue from evil."

Time will only admit of the consideration of one of these, and I select the first ; and I select it with a purpose. Probably all accredited teachers who are fortunate enough to minister to really thoughtful people have been interrogated as to a correspondence maintained in one of the daily papers under the heading, "Ought the clergy to criticize the Bible?" It is rather a foolish question, and might be met by the

Socratic method of further questioning. For
example :—

Ought the assimilative organs of the body to
criticize food ?

Ought the gold miners to criticize auriferous
ore ?

Ought the diamond polishers to criticize and
cut up the celebrated Premier diamond ?

Ought the human mind to estimate, and
value, and to criticize the successive self-revela-
tions of the Divine Originator, who seems to
encourage criticism in His exclamation, " Come
and let us reason together, saith the Lord "?

Ought the believer in the Christ revelation to
criticize the method and the meaning of the Holy
Incarnation, concerning which the Lord Himself
challenged criticism in His words, " What think
ye of the Christ ?"

But, wise or foolish, the question is before us,
" Ought the clergy to criticize the Bible ?" and
I contend that the words in this morning's
Gospel, " Launch out into the deep," give the
reply clearly and decisively in the affirmative.
How, for example, could we arrive at a right
understanding of the words of this morning's
Gospel, unless we brought to bear upon them
the critical faculty ? Scripture is fatally im-
poverished by being interpreted on the plane of
shallow, superficial literalism. In this history
to-day a searching, critical intelligence looks
behind and beyond the surface beauty of the

Oriental picture, beyond the natural scenery of the lake district of Palestine, the blue waters of the Sea of Galilee, the fertile plains of Gennesaret, dotted with the figures of the eager listeners crowding round the improvised pulpit on the shore, and criticism, esoteric criticism, the highest criticism, fixes upon the spiritual interpretation of the eternal injunction of the Incarnate Lord as, with the whole world in His thoughts, with you and me in His thoughts, He says, " Launch out into the deep." In your eager desire to know God, let down your nets of criticism and inquiry into those still depths where first principles and changeless laws lie hid ; and, though the un-explored and the unthinkable will always still remain, you will have thought yourself far beyond the sphere of shallow controversy into the bosom of the Universal Parent Spirit, and that is home. Thus intelligent criticism becomes the pathway to spiritual discovery.

" Ought the clergy to criticize the Bible," supposing, of course, that they are qualified by scholarship and application ? Let us first con-sider what we understand by the Bible. The Bible represents one form of the activity of the Eternal Reason or Self-utterance of God, which is called the " Word." The first great Bible was, of course, the universe, the Word expressing itself in matter. The Eternal has written His history with the pen of patient time upon the strata of the globe. Thousands of investigators have criticized this Bible, and, like Mr. Herbert Spencer, have, as the result of their criticism, read in it the scientific necessity of an "infinite and eternal energy from whom all things proceed." But this is not the Bible the controversialists mean. They mean the written records claiming to reveal to men in different ages such measure of the thought-transcending plans of God as in each age men were able and ready to receive. Ought the clergy to criticize that Bible? That Bible is not a book; it is a literature, consisting of sixty-seven books, by many different authors, extending over many ages, consisting of history, poetry, prophecies, laws, and morals. It in no sense professes to be a finished disclosure of final truth, but a record of the gradual self-revelation of the secrets of the Lord, revealed through the minds of men of very different mental endowments and spiritual apprehensions, whose idiosyncracies of mind and character were not overruled by the inspiring Spirit of God.

No literary compilation that has ever been given to the world has been subjected to such rigorous, ceaseless, remorseless criticism as the Bible. Its existence has begun, continued, and has progressed in criticism. As the late Lord Salisbury said in his address at the centenary of the British and Foreign Bible Society, any other literature subjected to criticism so destructive would have long since passed away.

Its survival is one of its guarantees, and one of
the credentials of its inspiration. The miracle
of the book is greater than any miracle *in* the
book. Yes, that blessed volume lying on the
lectern of the church is the outcome, the product of the machinery called criticism. A
majority of the yeas and nays of thoughtful
human critics have from time to time decided
what books should be included and what rejected from the canon of Scripture.

What is the history of the growth of our
Bible ? Briefly, the beginning of our present
collection called the Bible was made by Ezra,
who, in the fifth century before Christ, repub-
lished the five books called the Pentateuch, and
designated them " The holy book of the Jewish
people." After him Nehemiah added the books
of Joshua, Judges, Samuel, and Kings ; and at
the same time the third group of Old Testament
Scriptures, called the Hagiographa, or sacred
writings, were gathered by an unknown hand.
Professor Westcott, afterwards Bishop of Durham,
tells us that the canon of Old Testament Scriptures was formed gradually during a lengthened
interval, beginning with Ezra, from B.C. 458 to
332. At the time of our Lord there were two
distinct collections of Old Testament writings,
one in Hebrew, the other a translation into the
Greek, made by the Jews in Alexandria, called
the Septuagint, and which contained the Apo-
crypha. The Septuagint was the Scripture used

by our Lord and the Apostles, and it is from the Septuagint that the quotations from the Old Testament found in the New Testament are taken. The actual shape of our Old Testament as we now possess it was practically settled at the Synod of Jamnia, A.D. 90, and was reconsidered and resettled at the Council of Carthage, in 397, presided over by Augustine.

Our New Testament has a similar, though briefer history. The earliest list, made in the year 170, mentions all the books we now possess except the Epistle to the Hebrews, the Epistles of Peter, and the Epistle of James. For over two hundred years various lists of books were compiled by such men as Clement of Alexandria, Tertullian, Origen, and Eusebius, some rejecting books we now receive as canonical, others admitting books that are now rejected, until, at the Council of Carthage, in 397, our New Testament was finally fixed in its present form.

Thus did men, exercising the critical faculty in the Councils of the Church, give us our Bible in its present shape ; and he who denies that the Holy Spirit guided the deliberations of the critics in the Council of Carthage has no guarantee of the authenticity of his Bible, beyond his own private judgment, which may lead him, as it led Luther, to deny the inspiration of the Epistle of St. James, and to consider the revelation of St. John as on a level with the book of Esdras, which Luther said he should like to toss into the Elbe.

But, obviously, the critics at the Council of Carthage cannot be considered to have uttered the last word as to the composition of the Bible. We are told that we shall know if we " follow on " to know the Lord. We do not work now by œcumenical councils. In our own generation, reverent-minded scholars, historians, and investigators have continued the work, and have been " following on " to know the Word of the Lord. Three kinds of criticism have been applied to the Scriptures :—

1. *The lower criticism*, which concerns itself simply with the state of the text, discovering and eradicating errors and interpolations.

2. *The higher criticism*, which is scholastic and intellectual, and concerns itself with the composition, authorship, date, and historic value of the sacred books.

3. *The highest criticism*, which is intuitive and esoteric, exercising the discriminating faculty to discover, beneath allegory, parable, and variation, the self-revelation of the mind and will of God.

What has been the effect of this criticizing, this probing, this eager desire to separate husk from wheat, upon the Old Testament, upon the New Testament, upon the theory of inspiration ? Briefly, very briefly, it has been this. As to the Old Testament : the Old Testament is practically declared to be a stately, simple, monotheistic recapitulation, under Divine inspiration, of a vast literature, which extended over the Oriental world from the most remote epoch. This is elaborated in Professor Sayce's valuable work, called "The Higher Criticism and the Monuments." The *form* of the various parts of the Old Testament is as distinct from its *substance* as the form of a grain of wheat is distinct from the life-germ within it. The spiritual man will discover, accept, and assimilate the consummate beauty of the progressive self-revelation of God without troubling himself as to the inaccuracies of transcribers, the mental peculiarities of writers, or doubtful historical statements, exactly as the assimilative organs of the body discriminate between food that can be built into the system and food that must be cast out into the draught. The spiritual digestive faculty, for example, will feed upon a glorious utterance like that of Isaiah, "Doubtless Thou art our Father, our Redeemer from everlasting is Thy name," while it casts out into the draught the story of Elisha, and the children, and the she bears. And, from the criticism of the Old Testament, we have learnt the unity of all religions, the common Divine origin of man, the slow, patient evolution of God's self-revelation.

And as to the New Testament, what have we gained? Conclusions of inestimable value. The New Testament consists of four biographical sketches; one narrative of the work of some missionary teachers; twenty-one letters, six of

6

them addressed to individuals; and one description of a heavenly vision. The four biographical sketches have been severely tested in the crucible of scientific criticism, and have been proved to be documents of the first century of a high order of historical accuracy. No one now dare commit himself to the satetment that they are worthless forgeries of a later date. The authorship of the Gospel of St. Mark, A.D. 65, compiled from reminiscences of St. Peter, is absolutely undisputed; the Gospel of St. John, though its date and authorship are still an open question, contains the proof within itself that God's Spirit gave it for the light and guidance of mankind; the book of the Acts has been proved to be certainly the work of the author of the third Gospel; and the letters of St. Paul are accepted as genuine by the greatest scholars with practical unanimity. Thus the diamond comes back to us from the hands of the polishers, smaller if you will, but more brilliant and more valuable. In the indisputable portion of the New Testament, the Gospel of St. Mark, and the Pauline letters, we have the authentic life of the Christ and the history of the growth of Christian doctrine—a revelation which gives us the Holy Incarnation, the Holy Eucharist, the identification of the Risen Christ with His brethren, and the organization of the Church.

And one point more. Modern criticism has widened our conception of inspiration. Inspiration is (1) Universal; (2) Special. All special inspirations are specimens, divinely provided, to call the attention of men to universal inspiration. Inspiration is the inward action of God's Universal Spirit expressing itself in everything. We are told that Bezaleel was inspired when he cut the precious stones and wove the coverings for the tabernacle. Would you deny the same inspiration to Michael Angelo, to Benvenuto Cellini, to Torrigiano? Special inspirations, I repeat, are specimens of universal inspiration. For example:

Jesus is the specimen and guarantee of the Divine Sonship of the race.

Sunday is the specimen and guarantee that all days are the Lord's.

The Eucharist is the specimen and guarantee of the universal presence of the Risen Lord.

The Bible is the specimen and guarantee of the Divine purpose behind all books that are noble, true, and inspiring.

And, lastly, all revelation, whether in nature, humanity, or literature, is intended to lead us to one glorious all-diffused individuality, manifested and interpreted in the Incarnation, and whose dwelling-place is the heart of man.

"Sanctify this," says St. Peter, in to-day's Epistle, sanctify this Christ nature, this indweller, this potential germ of the Divine, "in your hearts as Lord." Acknowledge, co-operate with this mystic, hidden, Divine vitality. Let

6—2

it live its life in you, let it think its thoughts in
you, and it will enrich the poverty of your
efforts, elevate the scope of your life, ensuring
you irrevocably in this world increasing knowledge of God's truth, and in the world to come
life everlasting.

THE SABBATH.

" There is one body, and one Spirit."—*Eph*. iv. 3.

ALL right-minded persons, all who keenly sympathize with those who live by labour, all who love and pity the burden-bearing animals other than man, will rejoice at the influential movement now in progress in connection with the due observance of Sunday. It is a fact positively calculated to cause joy amongst the angels of God that the representatives of the various conflicting sects of Christendom should at last have discovered a cause, noble, inspiring, utilitarian, which can unite them cordially upon the same platform.

Now, while we are deeply thankful for this recrudescence of a national recognition of the sanctity and privileges of the Christian Sunday, it cannot be out of place to inquire as to the origin and the obligation of the day of rest. And the thought which seems to me to underlie the all-embracing declaration, " There is one body, and one Spirit," suggests to my own mind the solution of the conundrum once proposed by our Lord to the Scribes and Pharisees connected with Sabbath obligation. They were "watching Him," and He answered their thought with the question, "Is it lawful to heal on the Sabbath day?" And we read, "They held their peace." They were wise to hold their peace. The question was one which could not be settled either by Sabbatarian bigotry on the one hand or by atheistic irresponsibility on the other. It demanded thought, combined with wisdom and historic knowledge, and a wider conception of the Infinite Spirit of God than the Jewish theology provided. The axiom which is immutable, and by which all problems may be tested, is this, "There is one body, and one Spirit." God has never changed. "I am the Lord," He says; "I change not." God has ever been, ever will be, the "one Spirit," the whole unity, the sum total, of what we understand by "spirit"; "Above all, through all, in all." The progressive self-revelation of the nature of God does not imply any change in God; the change is in man's capacity for apprehending God. Whatever the God-conceptions of the different ages of the world have been, the "one body" has always been the universe—varied, wonderful, glorious. The "one Spirit" has always been God; infinite, unsearchable, all-containing. The "body" has always been full filled by "the Spirit." Though the Spirit has expressed itself in a diversity of ways and degrees in different things, it has always been the same. One intelligence has always dominated all things, from the least unto the greatest. In the crystal, the flower, the tree, the bird, the beast, the man, the "one Spirit" has ever been present, expressing Himself, revealing Himself, so far and so far only as He could be profitably apprehended by the mental standard of each age of the world's history. There is, and there ever has been, "one body, and one Spirit."

And how, you ask, does this axiom imply the answer to our Lord's question ? It is in this way. The problem suggested was Sabbath observance, and the lawfulness of certain acts on the Sabbath day. It is an important problem both from the religious and the social point of view. It is now once more prominently before us, and the different bodies, social and religious, who are exploiting the subject would give very different reasons for the observance of the day. Let us ask the question, What is the obligation of Sabbath observance ; is it legal, or religious, or both, or neither ; and whence does it arise ? The most usual and the most conventional reply is that it arises from the fourth commandment in the Decalogue, which we read every Sunday in our churches. Is that so ? Does the Sabbath come from the Decalogue ? Look at the 20th chapter of the Book of Exodus and the 8th verse. The words are, "*Remember* the Sabbath day." This is the only commandment which commences with the

word " remember." The word " remember " implies reference to something past which has been
neglected or forgotten ; its use here implies
that the Sabbath was not an obligation then for
the first time enforced, but an ancient institution,
long anterior to the vision on Mount Sinai, now
to be recalled to memory and emphasized. How
far back in the distant past can we trace the
institution of the Sabbath ? It is not easy even
for the expert historian to give a positive answer
to the question. Our knowledge is gained from
the clay tablets, some of which are in the British
Museum, which have been exhumed from very
ancient royal libraries in the temples and palaces
of Chaldea, and which have been deciphered
since Dr. Young, whose memorial tablet is in
Westminster Abbey, with wonderful patience and
ingenuity, translated the inscription on the
Rosetta stone. From these clay tablets the
institution of the Sabbath, and the name " Sabbath," are, according to Mr. S. Laing in his
interesting work on " Human Origins," con-
clusively proved to have been in existence more
than one thousand years before the convention-
ally accepted Biblical date of the creation of the
world, and therefore at least three thousand
years before the law was given on Mount Sinai.
Probably the oldest of these tablets was inscribed not less than ten thousand years ago,
and some of them contain the names of the days
of the week to which we still adhere (the Quakers,

I believe, are the only community which has rejected them, and speak of first day, second day, and so on), connecting the names of the days with the names of the planets, which were considered to be gods influencing human events. From this naming the days according to the planets arose the fact and the name of Sabbath. Saturday, the Sabbath, was Saturn's day, the day on which Saturn's influence was considered to be paramount. Saturn was thought to be the oldest, the most malignant, the most feared of these mythological planetary deities ; it was therefore considered by these Accadian astrologers, the ancient inhabitants of Chaldea, most perilous to do any work or to commence any undertaking on the Sabbath, Saturn's day, or Saturday, and the rules of the most rigid Sabbatarian strictness were enforced in ancient Babylon and Nineveh in order to avert public calamity. One very ancient inscription enumerates the duties of a king, and he is positively forbidden to drive in his chariot, to put on clean linen, to eat cooked food, or even to take medicine on the Sabbath, Saturn's day, lest he should provoke the anger of the malignant planetary deity. This primitive, deeply-rooted superstition as to the unluckiness of Saturn's day, though common to most ancient nations, was specially powerful in Chaldea, and from thence it descended to the Semite races who succeeded the Chaldeans. Abraham, the founder of the Jewish race, was born and educated in Chaldea in " Ur of the Chaldees," and he would naturally have clung tenaciously to the conception of Saturn's day, retaining it even when the gradual self-revelation of the world's Creator had supplanted these lower conceptions of astrological deities with the higher conception of Jahveh or Jehovah. Thus the obligation of the Sabbath as the one day in the seven on which no work was to be done, and nothing was to be undertaken, was gradually elevated from the evil day of Saturn to the holy day of Jehovah, and while the Chaldean name " Sabbath " was retained, a nobler, gentler reason was given for observing the day. The reason given in the Decalogue, and to this day retained, was based upon the prevailing conception that God made the world in six days by a kind of " mechanical engineer " process, and then rested on the seventh day. It was a better reason than the Chaldeans' reason, but still it was a reason obviously accommodated to their mental condition at the time as recipients of the new monotheistic conception of God as the one sole Creator of the world. When, many years afterwards, the Jews, placing ceremony before charity, and religious externalism before righteousness, blamed our Lord for doing good on the Sabbath, He practically abolished this reason in a single sentence : " My Father," He said, " worketh hitherto, and I work." " Worketh " implying continuity. It

is as though He had said: the expression as to
God resting from creating was a verbal accommodation for rudimentary minds. If God really what
you call " rested," in other words, stayed the
activity of His ever-active, ever-evolving Spirit,
even for the fraction of a second, the universe
would become chaos. " My Father worketh
hitherto, and I work." There is no Sabbath, no
one day's rest in seven, to the Omnipotent Self-
Evolver who was manifested in Jesus.

The evolution of this Accadian Sabbath, this
Saturn's unlucky day, through the Jewish Sabbath
into the Christian Sunday, was obvious and simple.
The early Christian Church, whether wisely or
unwisely is questionable, in their earnest desire
to elevate Pagan worship, adopted, as far as
possible, the sacred days of the older cults, and
grafted on to them Christian commemorations.
Thus for Christmas Day they adopted December
25, which was the festival of Bacchus, when the
Romans celebrated the Saturnalia; though the
simplest calculation from the date of the course
of Abijah to the birth of John the Baptist, and
from that to the birth of the Child of Mary,
will show that our Lord was born, not in December, but in June. At first the Christian Church
observed both Saturday, Saturn's day, the day
which had been adopted by the Hebrews, and
Sunday, the new day, the Christian day, as
days of rest. In the reign of Constantine Saturday was abolished, and the whole observance

was concentrated upon Sunday as the day commemorating the Lord's first appearance after His crucifixion, and it was named the Lord's day, *Dies Dominica*, or, as in France, *Dimanche*.

Now, what does this historical investigation, so ably worked out by Mr. Laing, prove ? Does it destroy the legal obligation and the religious aspect of Sunday ? The legal obligation, perhaps ; the religious aspect, certainly not. On the contrary, it greatly emphasizes it and places it upon a sure basis. But, you say, these students of the clay tablets have traced the origin of our Sunday observance to the absurd superstition of Accadian astrologers of 7,000 years ago ! They have ; but my answer is : " There is, there always has been, ' one body,' the universe and all that is in it ; and ' one Spirit,' God, the soul of the universe." What you perhaps justly stigmatize as the absurd superstition of Accadian astrologers was the upward yearning of human hearts, the differentiated Divinity in man seeking the universal Divinity whence it came ; feeling after the great unknown in response to the very gradual unveiling of the profound relation of the Creative Soul to the human race. These Accadian astrologers of 7,000 years ago were the highest thinkers of the " one body " of that particular period ; immanent in that " one body " was the " one Spirit " expressing Himself rudimentarily, tentatively, always having " many things to say which they could not then bear."

Their inadequate superstitious notion of Saturn and his unlucky day was all the interpretation which they could at that time apply to the mystic pressure of the "one Spirit," which, moving with the majestic slowness of its wont, was establishing for the "one body," the whole world, an institution of universal religion, obviously in harmony with the requirements of human nature. In the childhood of the world the conception of the day of rest was at its lowest level of motive, namely, the avoidance of ill fortune. In its higher evolution it became the religious obligation of the Decalogue, suited to a race first entering upon Monotheism; thence it grew into the Christian Sunday; and the very superstitions of the past which have clung to it, as a morsel of eggshell will cling to the newly-hatched bird, have, as Mr. Laing truly says, proved a powerful means of preserving this blessed day of rest through all the social and political revolutions of race progress, and millions of toilers now enjoy a rest and recreation on one day in seven because Accadian astrologers 7,000 years ago were afraid of the malignant influence of the planet Saturn. But it was the secret stirring of the "one Spirit" that prompted these Accadian representatives of the "one body" to rest from all labour on the Sabbath day.

Do you express surprise that God should have allowed Himself to be so misunderstood, so inadequately conceived, as to be mistaken for the planet Saturn? Why be surprised? Is He not misunderstood now? Do you really imagine that the more intimate and paternal conception that we have received through the Christian Revelation is exhaustive and final, that there is no more to know? Will not our present names, conceptions, analyses, and definitions of God, wholly adequate as they are for our present needs, appear as childish and imperfect when we reach the sphere where we shall " know even as we are known," as the superstitions of the Accadians appear to us now? Jesus, the interpreter of God, warned us that the Father was greater than He. It is as if He had said: " Though I present to you as perfect a conception of the Universal Father-Spirit as you can now receive, there is much more to know, for the Absolute, the ' one Spirit,' is greater even than the very highest of His possible manifestations."

This, then, is the point to which we have arrived: the obligation of Sunday does not rest upon the fourth commandment, but is an obligation of universal religion which from the earliest days has been dimly perceived, and which has been maintained always, everywhere, by all. Its sanction is therefore infinitely more solemn and more directly Divine than if it had in reality been initiated amidst the thunders of Mount Sinai; and the due observance of Sunday can never be secured by penal clauses in Acts of Parliament, or by quoting the fourth commandment and telling men that God will punish them if they break it. There is no such sin in the Christian revelation as " Sabbath-breaking." The idea and the name belong to the days of the Accadian astrologers. The law of love will solve all the problems connected with Sunday observance, and nothing else will. To the man whose interior relation to the Lord and to humanity is right the question will ever be, not What is lawful ? but What is good ? What is most beneficial for our soul's progress, our neighbour's happiness, and the welfare of the community at large ? Sunday observance becomes, therefore, a matter of individual conscience. If your conscience is under the conception of the Accadian, or the Jew, or the English Puritan who " hanged his cat on Monday for killing of a mouse on Sunday," be a strict Sabbatarian until your mental horizon is expanded. If your conscience is based on the law of love, love to God and love to your neighbour, you will decide for yourselves what you may or may not do on the *Dies Dominica*, the Lord's Day. And as the Advisory Committee appointed by the Archbishop wisely says : " The only remedy for the non-observance of Sunday is a general renewal of Christian ideals, and the education of public opinion by means of a fearless and well-informed proclamation of the true principles upon which the Christian observance of the Lord's Day must be founded, and by a simultaneous and united appeal to the conscience of the nation." Yes, conscience is the final court of appeal. Doubtless all are familiar with the legend as to our Lord's utterance to the man who was gathering sticks on the Sabbath day : " If thou knowest, O man, what thou art doing, blessed art thou ; if thou knowest not, thou art a law-breaker and accursed." The key to the whole question is in our Lord's declaration, " The Sabbath was made for man "; that is, it was designed and prescribed by a loving Father for man's welfare and happiness in this infant school of earthly life, in which he is being educated, sanctified, perfected, prepared for the eternal rest that " remaineth for the people of God "; and the people of God, remember, are not a select and privileged few, but the totality of the members of the human race, in all ages, everywhere, and always, for

" THERE IS ONE BODY, AND ONE SPIRIT."

NELSON AND TRAFALGAR.

" Thou shalt keep him in perfect peace whose mind is stayed
on Thee."—*Isaiah* xxvi. 3.

THE margin of the R.V. paraphrases the
word " mind " by the word " imagination," and the paraphrase is suggestive, for the
trained use of the imagination is a valuable
factor in the realm of spiritual apprehension,
and it is to the imagination that I shall appeal
to-day. The Divine programme for a restful
heart amidst the insoluble problems and perpetual paradoxes of human education is a maintained attitude of the imagination trained to
pierce through all second causes, and rest in
the one Infinite originating cause which is, and
which logically must be, the producer, the sus-
tainer, and the ruler of the universe and all
that is in it.

Do any, I wonder, share with me a sense of
being confronted with a paradox in connection
with the Nelson Centenary ? On the one hand,
as professing recipients of the Christian revelation, we are under the obligation to condemn
war, with all its unspeakable horrors, as in-
herently iniquitous in itself and in its effects

7

upon the race, and as an insolent defiance of
the teaching of the Christ, who brands the killing
of our brother men as murder and fratricide.
On the other hand, we are called upon as patriotic
Englishmen to unite in a widespread national
movement of praise and thanksgiving for the
crowning mercy of the sanguinary naval victory
of Trafalgar one hundred years ago, when our
glorious Nelson and some two thousand Englishmen, and nearly twice as many Frenchmen,
laid down their lives in the strenuous endeavour
to slay one another. Is there not some mental
embarrassment in this paradox ? The simple
mind wishes to know how it can adjust and
harmonize apparent contradictories ; how it
can religiously dedicate regimental colours, con-
secrate with prayer and benediction iron-clad
engines of destruction, make a sacred fetish of
tattered banners, thank God for success in killing
our fellow men, and still profess discipleship to
Him who taught the unity of humanity and
the inseverabliity of God and man in the words,
" I in them and Thou in Me, that they may be
made perfect in one."

I think the sense of embarrassment arises from
the difficulty of emancipating our minds from the
rudimentary conventional Deistic conception of
God, and from the unwillingness of the human
mind to rest in the profounder, more universal
conception of God as the Omnipotent Spirit of
evolution—above all, in all, and through all :

slowly advancing to ultimate perfection a universe in which He has expressed Himself for an
inextinguishable and glorious purpose. The distinction between Creation and Evolution is as
wide as the poles. Creation, the idea that a
creative will, with no limits to its power, built
up worlds and their contents by some omnipotent mechanical operation, interposes an immeasurable chasm between the Creator and that
which is created. The profound conception of
Divine evolution sees God, not as an objective
localised Person, but as a Supreme Intelligence
everywhere, in every thing, out of which all
individual forms of existence are constantly
emerging. To the evolutionist creation is not
an action effected once for all, but a continuous
process, the tireless activity of the Divine immanence. " My Father," said Jesus, " worketh."
" In Him," said St. Paul, " all things consist ";
every sprouting seed, every wheeling planet,
every ordinary movement of the natural world,
every noble aspiration of the human heart is
an evidence of the energy of the ever-present,
ever-active Soul of the universe. Why is this
conception of God as the vitally Real Presence
everywhere, the generative and animating power
in everything, unrecognized, unwelcomed ? Because, from the very first, the teaching of the
Christ was overlaid with the Hebrew conception
which nationalized God, and with the non-
Hebrew Deism which localized God on a throne
outside His universe.   7—2

The whole scheme of Western Augustinian theology, of which the modern Church is the inheritor, turns upon this hypothesis of an external, localized God. This externalizing of God, this localizing of the Universal Soul in a distant heaven, though obviously an accommodation permitted to the mind of man in a rudimentary stage, on his way from Polytheism to Monotheism, is pregnant with difficulty, and originates the paradoxes which embarrass devout minds.

If He is ruling the world from outside, occasionally interfering with the resistless play of forces which He originally set in motion, how difficult it is to screen our loving Heavenly Father in human thought from the imputation of bad government. Why is there not more interference with the crimes, the brutalities, the hideous degradations of His human subjects? The human mind tentatively and inquiringly and reverently says to itself, either this external localized world-ruler is not wholly good, a paralyzing conception which destroys every standard of morality; or He is not wholly omnipotent, which burdens the mind with the perplexity of dualism; or He is wholly good and wholly omnipotent, but not wholly wise, which is a *reductio ad absurdum*.

Does the Christian revelation of God afford relief to this perplexed mental attitude? Does it contribute a conception of God upon which the mind can be stayed so as to be kept in perfect peace? Does it unveil a representation of the Eternal more reverent, more rational, more attractive than a sterile Deism which banishes God from the world, or a reactionary Pantheism which loses Him in it? As I understand it, the creed of the Christ was that God is Spirit; not even *a* Spirit, as it is wrongly rendered, but Spirit; the eternal, self-existent essence whose name, and the law of whose being, is love; that creation is this love expressing itself in all forms of creaturely activity, the highest of which is humanity; that God is not therefore a Person, but an all-diffused Individuality, self-conscious in all things and all men; that though not a Person, inasmuch as He is the life-propagator, He may be estimated and addressed by us as Father, that we may say to Him, " Our Father which art in heaven," " Our Infinite Universal Parent Spirit, Thou art everywhere, the pulsation of Thy life through all things causes all to live and move and have their being"; and that, if the mental demand for Personality in the Universal Parent Soul becomes at any time paramount, it can be fully satisfied by adoration of the one unique Personality in whom the fulness of the moral character of the universal soul was embodied, for Jesus is the Sacrament of the Absolute, the outward and visible sign of the inward and spiritual individuality of the all-diffused being whom we call God.

This is what I understand by the Christian revelation of God ; and, to my own mind, this conception of God as the Omnipotent Spirit of evolution, slowly advancing mankind to a more and ever more perfect condition, relieves the sense of paradox, and minimises the feeling of surprize at the presence and power of what we call moral and physical evil in the world.

The relief comes in this way. Even God can only make things by means of the process by which they become what they are ; evolution is a gradual process, and the law of its working is progressive victory over contradiction ; goodness would have no significance in the conscious life of man without its contrast by which to recognize it. Therefore, the unrest, and the disorder, and the suffering, and the imperfection in the world are not due to bad ruling from outside, but to the nature and the conditions of the slow, but ultimately irresistible, process of evolution from within ; they arise from immaturity, leading to perverted and defective volition ; from humanity's present stage of only partial development ; from man's incapacity as yet to realize the truth unfolded by the Christ which we see as the perfect ideal, namely, man's absolute oneness with God. Meanwhile, the Divine evolution slowly but irresistibly progresses, and one of its products is civilization in the sense of justice, equity, and equal rights ; and in this plane of its work it meets its oppositions and

pushes through them ; it comes from time to
time into sharp collision with grasping tyrannies,
and corrupt social conditions, and unbounded
ambitions, like those of Napoleon, and times
and circumstances must arise in the process of
race-development when war is inevitable and
hideous death struggles are the result ; and the
heroes who, with no personal bitterness, take
the lives of others and lay down their own lives
are, in the profound inwardness of things, unconscious instruments of this self-evolving *anima
mundi*, who is above all, and through all, and in
all, and whom we address as " Our Father which
art in heaven." But whilst hating, deprecating,
opposing evil in all its developments, if we are
Evolutionists rather than Creationists, we may
be absolutely certain of the temporary, pro-
visional, relative, evanescent character of that
resisting agency of evolution that we call evil.
We may rest in the assurance that pain, sorrow,
struggle, war are, in our immature state, the
inevitable travail pains of the birth of a nobler
life for the race, the sicknesses of humanity's
childhood, the excreta of the growing human
race, existing, not in spite of, but as an ingredient of, the emergence of the true life of
humanity which, when realized and experienced,
will enable us to say with St. Paul, " I reckon
that the sufferings of this present time are not
worthy to be compared with the glory that shall
be revealed in us."

I am, therefore, quite consistently able to thank God for the sanguinary victory of Trafalgar one hundred years ago, and to recognize that, though such terrible incidents are part of the crash of the machinery of a world still in the making, and far from the ideal of the finished product, there are on the surface plane, the plane of second causes, reasons for thankfulness and lessons to be learned.

For example : Trafalgar secured for Britain the command of the seas ; Trafalgar enabled Britain to colonize and civilize and bring the blessings of good government to a large portion of the world ; Trafalgar made possible much missionary enterprize, by which the knowledge of the Christ has been carried far and wide.

Again, if unmurmuring resignation, obliteration of social distinctions, unflinching fortitude, and complete unselfishness are fruits of the Spirit, then this painful product of the secret evolving force of the universal intelligence called war—horrible, barbarous as it is—works for good by raising the standard of a nation's life, and awakening characteristics apt to be stifled by luxury and selfishness in an atmosphere of indolent peace.

Then how remarkable a character study is afforded by our glorious hero, Nelson. He was not an ascetic. It would be an easy task for the critical moralist to put his finger on certain irregularities, of the seriousness of which, however, God is the only true judge. Of Nelson's brilliant achievements, his priceless services to the nation, of what is called the "magic of his touch," there is no need to speak; they are acknowledged by the civilized world, and have been the theme of glowing eulogies in the press; but as a study in human psychology Nelson stands almost alone. He was a unique combination of characteristics rarely gathered into a single personality: undaunted courage with feminine tenderness, dogged assurance with true personal humility, enthusiastic patriotism with a perfectly childlike trust in God. This tenderness of heart and perfect self-abandonment to the will and purpose of God are touchingly illustrated by that extract from his diary when he left the home that he loved to take command, for what proved to be the last time, of the fleet: "At half-past 10 drove from dear, dear Merton, where I left all which I hold dear in this world, to go to serve my King and my country. May the great God whom I adore enable me to fulfil the expectations of my country; and if it is His good pleasure that I should return, my thanks will never cease being offered up to the throne of His mercy. If it is His good providence to cut short my days on earth, I bow with the greatest submission, relying that He will protect those dear to me that I may leave behind. His will be done. Amen."

And, whatever truth there may be in the

historic signal, "England expects every man to do his duty," amongst the recorded dying utterances of great men there is nothing nobler than his very last words : " Hardy, I know I am dying ; thank God, I have done my duty." How many of us will be able to say that at the moment of death ? And who can doubt that Nelson found the reward of duty when, in the cabin of the "Victory," he "awakened from the dream of life."

The crowning lesson of this conception of God, which de-localizes Him and recognizes Him as the inmost uplifting evolving life in all things, is profoundly solemn and intensely practical. If He is immanent even in these struggles of race development, do I dare to doubt that He is immanent in myself ? To that great discovery we must render the most watchful, prayerful, reverent culture. Our perfection, that which is spoken of as our salvation, is not, under this conception, a judicial decision from a great white throne in the distant future, or a Divine contrivance turning upon our accepting certain vicarious performances of another. It is the normal and progressive unfolding of the powers of our ideal humanity from which there can be no escape, and from which alone will emerge the life and beauty of the world to come, as the gorgeous butterfly emerges from the cater-pillar and the crysalis. Great is the responsi-bility of recognizing this most intimate relationship between God and man. The Christian revelation is God for us, God with us, God in us ; " the kingdom of heaven is within you." Great also is the consolation of knowing that this union between God and man is indissoluble. Here lies the basis for unfaltering assurance amidst the struggles, failures, disappointments, backslidings of this passing, perishing school time. The fact that I am is irrefragable proof that God the Father-Spirit has concerning me a purpose from all eternity ; and though we are often puzzled, blinded, baffled, dissatisfied, this thought is the silver lining to the darkest cloud of human life, for it is written :

" THOU SHALT KEEP HIM IN PERFECT PEACE WHOSE MIND IS STAYED ON THEE."

A PLEA FOR THE BISHOP OF LONDON'S FUND.

"They said unto Him, Master, where dwellest Thou? He saith unto them, Come and see."—*John* i. 38.

IS there any other reason, beyond those ever ready emotions of pity which all right minded people feel towards those who are in material need and spiritual destitution, is there any deeper reason why we should contribute all that we can afford, and more than we can afford, to the Bishop of London's fund, which labours for the bodily and spiritual uplifting of the lapsed masses of this vast city? I think there is, and I think it is discoverable in the inwardness, the esoteric interpretation behind the letter, of the incidents and sayings recorded in that portion of the immortal literature called the New Testament.

For example, who that understands anything of the methods of Oriental imagery imagines for a moment that the simple incident which I have quoted would have been recorded and preserved for two thousand years, and read and pondered by millions, if it merely meant, Come and see where I am lodging at Bethabara beyond Jordan?

Rabbi, where dwellest Thou ?

It is the profound question lying at the root of all the anxious inquiries into the life-producing powers of this wonderful universe.

Where dwellest Thou ?—Thou who art the specific embodiment in one human Personality of that all inclusive Logos, or Word, or self-utterance of the Infinite Originator, by Whom all things were made.

Where dwellest Thou ?   Hast Thou a throne, a dwelling-place, a home, remote, inaccessible ? Art Thou abiding in some distant spot in the universe ?   Theologians speak of Thee as abiding somewhere locally, at a point in space which is termed God's right hand ;   an absent Lord, far away, beyond the shining of the farthest star, and that some day Thou wilt come again to the planet Thou hast deserted, in glorious majesty.   Where, where dwellest Thou ?

Note well His answer :   " Come and see." Effort is implied ;   bestir thyself, experimentalize, analyze, investigate, think, follow out clues, draw inferences.   There is a faculty within thee called spiritual discernment ;   it is connected with all the other powers of thy complex being and yet distinct from them all.   It is influenced by love, conscience, reverence, aspiration—all of them natural powers ;   yet it has a sphere of its own.   Use it, exercise it, open it ;   it is thy inward vision.   " Come and see."

What is the first inference from this coming

and seeing where He dwells ?   The first characteristic of inward vision is that it sees and knows
a truth, not in its particular, but in its universal
aspect.   Where doth He dwell ?   Ask the author
of the fourth Gospel ;   he says, " Without Him
was not anything made that was made, and
that which was made was life in Him." Life
in Him ; then He is the one Infinite life, the
universal, all-pervading, uplifting life.   There is
one body, the illimitable universe ; and one
Spirit, the penetrating life thereof.   Then the
first answer given by spiritual vision to the
question, " Where dwellest Thou ?" is everywhere ; immanent in all worlds, conscious in all
atoms, self-realizing in every electrode.   Yes,
there is a sense true and irrefragable, and completely free from Pantheism, in which the whole
wondrous universe is His dwelling-place, and
the ceaseless reproducing generative power which
throbs in every blade of grass and uplifts every
seed is the expression of His immanent and
active presence.   The utterance that Goethe
puts into the mouth of the earth spirit in
" Faust "—

> Thus at the roaring loom of time I ply,
> And weave for God the garments that thou seest Him by,

is true of Him.   The real earth spirit is the
Logos, the self-utterance of the Absolute, embodied for purposes of observation in Jesus.   I
know that thus to say He dwells everywhere is,
to the unopened vision, a perplexity tantamount

to saying that He dwells nowhere, for universal
diffusion is, to the average mind, unthinkable.
The Incarnation is the relief to this perplexity,
for in Jesus we can find and love and worship
the Logos as a Person ; moreover, He has ten-
derly provided the outward forms of worship
of the visible Church, in which His Presence
is promised and guaranteed, and specially in
the appointed sacrament of the Holy Eucharist,
the peculiar channel of communion or com-
munication between His universal Presence and
the hearts of His brethren on earth. But these
are accommodations to the weakness of our
finite condition. Even Augustine, the arch-
enemy of winged thought, has said the sacra-
ments are of the night, not of the day ; and
the first clear, true answer to the question,
" Where dwellest Thou ?" is everywhere. And
if He dwelleth everywhere, it is only in metaphorical language that He can be said to come
and go, to ascend and descend. Thus the Ascension was not a local movement of a literal
body through trackless space, but a metaphorical
expression accommodated to our understanding.
The most thoughtful of the early fathers of the
Church clearly thus understood the Ascension
as the return of the peculiar embodiment of the
Eternal Logos to the central life, the Universal
Parent-life, whose outbreathed thought He was.
Justin Martyr says : " You are not to think
that the unbegotten came down from anywhere
and went up." And St. Chrysostom says, in

his homily against the Arians : " When the
Eternal Son is described as standing or sitting
at the right hand of God, these expressions are
not to be interpreted in a material sense, they
are expressions accommodated to our understanding." So, thank God, it is not necessary
to believe that the Ascension implies that He is
gone away from us to some local distance,
indescribable, unthinkable. He dwelleth everywhere.

But there is still a more accurate, a more
complete answer to the question, " Where
dwellest Thou ?" If you think that the immanence of the Logos everywhere sublimates
the Lord Christ away into vagueness, or buries
Him beneath the chaos of matter and force in
the natural world, then " come and see " a
little closer. The one life immanent in all,
through all, above all, expresses itself in different
degrees, and its highest expression on this planet
is Man. " Master, where dwellest Thou ?"
Everywhere—in mineral and crystal, and vegetable and animal, but above all in Man. Would
you indeed " come and see " where He specially
dwells ? Look within ; for as Faber says :

> Not alone in starry skies,
>   In vastness all abroad,
> But everywhere in every place
>   Abides the whole of God.
>
> For God is never so far off
>   As even to be near ;
> He is within, our spirit is
>   That which He holds most dear.

Obviously, it is not in the anatomy of the body that the true greatness of human life is discoverable. It is in the study and the analysis of the Ego, that centre in man which thinks, reasons, wills ; that self-consciousness that says I am I. That, though I cannot define it, is a differentiation of the Illimitable Soul, a fragment of the self-consciousness of the Logos. It is an expression of the Christ nature, His life in man, man's guarantee of eternal life ; and the true dwelling-place of Him who was specifically In-carnate as Jesus is human flesh and blood, the quivering, striving mass of the human race ; for Jesus was the specific embodiment of the Logos, or Word, which is immanent as the in-most life in every man ; and when I ask, solemnly and thoughtfully and expectantly, the question, " Where dwellest Thou ?" the true answer given by spiritual vision that has " come and seen " is : " I dwell in the inmost deepest being of man, as his central immortal Divine Sonship." This being so, when the Lord comes in glorious majesty to judge the quick and the dead, will it be by some visible appearance in the sky, or will it be by some opening of the spiritual faculty, as He came to John in Patmos, and some inward change in the heart ? What does He say Himself ? " When He was demanded of the Pharisees when the Kingdom of God should come, He answered them and said : The Kingdom of God cometh not with observation,

8

neither shall they say, Lo here, or Lo there, for, behold, the Kingdom of God is within you."

A penetrating apprehension of this transcendent answer to the question, " Where dwellest Thou ?" necessitates two inferences : the first, personal ; the second, general. The first, personal. In proportion as spiritual vision ripens, the standard of conduct will be changed, not as from without, but as from within ; the secret of human life is the " mystery hidden from the foundation of the world," the Christ in man. When realized—no, I will not say realized—but when the merest fringe of this profound truth of the interior relation between the Divine and the human is touched, life becomes a stricter, holier thing. A solemn mystery challenges you in the hour of temptation. To profane God's temple, to defile the home where the Master dwelleth, to suffer the traffickers to monopolize the holy of holies, is not error, but sacrilege. Gordon used to say, " I strive to live purely that my body may be a cleaner dwelling-place for the Lord." To offer to this indwelling mystery homage and watchful guardianship is to cultivate the energies whence character is formed. To know that Jesus is not only a model outside us, though He is that, but a vital force working within us, is to be lifted high above the conventional standards of theology, the rudimentary conceptions of sins, absolutions, penances, and so on, and to recognize that Christian character

is not a succession of meritorious deeds, which
are banked, as it were, to your account, but
the growth of an interior principle which will
automatically produce good actions as a tree
produces leaves. And the exhortation to cast
away the works of darkness and put upon us
the armour of light is the summons to awake
out of dreamland into the world of reality, to
be mentally immersed in that Soul of Souls
which is the interior eternal Kingdom of God
in man.

The second inference is general, and, if
accepted, will ensure a large offertory to-day.
The knowledge that the dwelling-place of the
Logos manifested in Jesus is Man will necessarily
influence your attitude towards others in your
home, in your business, in your social life ; you
will treat others honourably, courteously, up-
rightly, fraternally, as temples of the Lord.
Again, you will never despair of anyone ; the
Divine spark in man is the unshakable foundation of eternal hope for the Race. " Long sleeps
the summer in the seed," but it is there, and it
is inextinguishable. It was a mediæval custom
of the Benedictines, when a mendicant came to
beg, to imprint a kiss on his forehead. Whatever
the sores and defilement of that Lazarus, he was
the shrine of Deity. Again, you will understand
that this is the basis, the bed rock, the appeal,
as it is the element of hope, of every evangelistic
and remedial effort. Work amongst the lapsed

aims at awakening, at calling into activity a hidden power that is there, always there, even in the most degraded ; a power that can change, mould, and advance a life, combating the hindrance of environment and slowly building up character ; and you will recognize, appreciate, and cordially support the labour of unwearied compassion of the clergy, the lay missioners, the parochial visitors in connection with the Bishop of London's fund, who are devoting their whole lives " to rescue the perishing, care for the dying, to snatch them in pity from sin and the grave."

Of course, you will see that in a God inhabited humanity there ought not to be fallen men, and still less fallen women ; you will see with new eyes the sacrilege committed by anyone who leads a younger one into sin, or who by flattery, by stimulating the impulses of curiosity or affection, leads some woman into sin and condemns her to join that class of outcasts who haunt your streets like painted vampires. It is the dwelling-place of the Logos—the temple of God —that he has defiled, ruined, and destroyed. But the Divine nature within that victim is not dead ; the Christ, who when in embodiment never shrank from leper's touch or harlot's tear, is still there. " Master, where dwellest Thou ?" " Come and see," and you will discover Him in very unlikely dwelling-places. I have found His indwelling life in the most abandoned. Many are familiar with the story of the outcast who was found dead in a wretched garret in New York, friendless and starved. In her own handwriting, blotted with her tears, written just before her death, was found that pathetic wail, since reprinted by the thousand, of which these lines are a part :—

> Once I was pure as the snow but I fell,
> Fell like the snowflakes from heaven to hell,
> Fell to be trampled as filth on tne street,
> Fell to be scoffed at and spit on and beat.
> Pleading, cursing, dreading to die,
> Selling my soul to whoever would buy,
> Dealing in shame for a morsel of bread,
> Hating the living and fearing the dead.
> Merciful God, have I fallen so low ?
> And yet I was once like the beautiful snow.

Was not He, Whose name is love, still dwelling in that sad stricken heart ? " Master, where dwellest Thou ?" " Where sin is as scarlet, I am still there, and able to make once more the heart as white as snow."

Now this is the deeper reason to which I referred. It is the loving labour of these workers in connection with the Bishop of London's fund to find this chord in sin-polluted hearts and to set it vibrating once more. I don't trouble you with statistics and details. You may take it for granted that they are saving souls and bodies in London, and I plead with you to help God's lifeboat crew in this city. Associate yourselves by the liberality of your gifts with their remedial work, and do it from this, the highest, truest,

grandest standpoint : do it because you believe
that even in the most degraded there still abides
the salvable capacity, the germ of Divinity, the
potentiality of perfection, which is Christ in
humanity, the hope of glory.

JOINT HEIRS WITH CHRIST.

" Joint heirs with Christ."—*Rom.* viii. 16.

TO all who believe that the juxtaposition of the Altar Scriptures of any given Sunday is not accidental, but providential, the eighth Sunday after Trinity presents considerations full of boundless consolation and practical suggestions for the Christian life.

It would not be easy to discover a more luminous exposition of the three propositions which include the whole philosophy of life, namely, (1) the Divine over-rule, (2) the inherent sonship of the human race, and (3) the appointed method of individual education, than that which shines through the connection between the Collect, Epistle, and Gospel for to-day.

And first: the Divine over-rule. The Collect fills our mouths with words of glorious confidence in the Divine over-rule, emphasizing the responsibility of the Creating Spirit for every form of activity in the whole universe; acknowledging no ruler but the One Supreme Intelligence; addressing Him as " God, whose never-failing Providence orderest all things both

in heaven and on earth." No man, unless prepared to use language in a wholly non-natural
sense, can pray this prayer from any standpoint
save that of tranquil belief in the eternal and
resistless omnipotence of God. Either the
Church has put into his mouth the language of
delusion, or he is justified in believing that
God's infinite purpose can never be rendered
ultimately futile and abortive by the self-
conscious, self-determining obstinacy of finite
man. Whatever may be the blighting influence
of persistent aversion from God, if even one
solitary specimen of the human race were able
to stiffen himself by final impenitence into endless rebellion against Eternal Love, then God does
not " order all things both in heaven and on
earth." So, before we are called upon to consider
the responsibilities and privileges of sonship, the
ground is, as it were, cleared before us by the
Church's prayer, declaring that God's purpose,
immanent in human nature, will prove too strong
for all perversion. Based upon this proposition,
human life is transfigured, the " haunting oracles
that stir our clay " have lost their power to distress. The unanswerable problems, the harrowing
mysteries, the teasing memories, the irresistible
speculations, what do they signify if, with His
" unfailing Providence, God ordereth all things "?
God, the Universal Love-Force, the Absolute
Substance out of whom all individual forms of
existence are constantly emerging ; God, recog-

nized by the inextinguishable conscience of all
thinking men of all ages as Omnipotent, Responsible and Indivisible ; what does it really
signify by what name you call Him ?   On John
Addington Symonds' gravestone in Rome is
lettered the quotation from Cleanthes :—

> Lead Thou me, God, law, reason, motion, life,
> All names alike for Thee are vain and hollow.

I am, of course, fully aware that just here the
fretting shadow of the mystery of evil obtrudes
itself ; but the conclusion must not be eluded.
If He " ordereth all things," there can be no
everlasting rival to the one Author of the universe ; the whole mystery of evil, and all its
terrifying cross-working purposes, must be completely under the Divine over-rule, if He " ordereth all things."   While conscience cannot deny
the malignity of moral evil without dethroning
herself, to attempt to account for it upon the
supposition that there are two eternal elemental
principles, alongside each other, is perilously to
tamper with the very idea of God.   The majestic
declaration in Isaiah xlv. 6, " I am the Lord,
there is none else.   I form the light, and create
darkness : I make peace, and create evil : I
the Lord do all these things," authoritatively
obliterates the " two principles " superstition,
and there we may be well content to leave it.

And here follows the second of the great
propositions : the sonship of the human race.
The language of the Collect prepares the way

for the teaching of the Epistle. This "ordering all things" is not fatalism, the blind outworking of an impersonal, irrational force, but the Divine over-rule of a responsible Fatherly Providence. "The Spirit itself beareth witness with our spirit, that we are the children of God: and if children, then heirs; heirs of God, and joint heirs with Christ." Here the definition of God is enlarged. "God is Spirit." The definition of man is suggested. Man is spirit, because man is God's son. It is necessary to reiterate that an entire scheme of erroneous theology has emerged from the unfortunate selection of the word "adoption" as a translation of the Greek word "υἱοθεσία." This compound word (never used except in the Greek Testament) signifies the placing of one who was unconsciously a son into the knowledge of the fulness of his privileges, and it cannot be tortured into the meaning of our English word "adoption," which implies the receiving into a family of one who was not a son before, and training and educating him as though he were a son. Man is God's son, not because God has adopted him, but because man, in his inmost, is spirit. Pursue him through the chemical combinations of his bodily organism, track him through his automatic and influential systems, and there is ever a residuum, a somewhat, which eludes the investigator. What is this but Divine Spirit differentiated into separate human entities? What is this but the transmutation of God's thought into beings who think ? God and man must, then, come together, because of the affinity between them ; because the distinctive element of humanity is an emanation from the fulness of Divine life. Spirit is not a word that lends itself readily to definition, but it is the outbreathing of the inmost in God, and the inworking of the inmost in man. It is that part of man which is capable of living intercourse with God ; and he is the most God-like in whom it is most developed ; and where it is manifested in perfection, there is Divinity. The Divinity of Jesus is not, then, a theological dogma, but a logical necessity ; and what was positively true of Him is relatively true of all men. In their inmost nature men are differentiations of the breath of God, and the spirit of man abides in the Spirit of God, and the Spirit of God in the spirit of man, as the bird abides in the air, and the air in the bird. And "$\nu\iota o\theta\epsilon\sigma\iota a$," mistranslated " adoption," is the awakening of the inmost nature of man in response to the perpetual pleading and impact of the Spirit of God ; and the strange secret whisper of a higher life, the intuitive protest in the heart against unregulated animal appetites, the strong desire of the soul to mount upwards, these are not a collection of prejudices instilled in childhood, but rather the awakening of the intuitive ; deep calling unto deep ; the inmost faculty demanding God ; the Divine Spirit seeking to reveal son-

ship in us ; " the Spirit bearing witness with
our spirit, that we are the children of God."
When the pulse of this inmost Divine life has
once been felt, and the perception and affirmation of sonship has once stirred within, though
it may be tentative, shadowy, indefinable, it
can never be argued away ; though it may be
ignored, resisted, silenced, it takes its place
henceforth in that life as a mental fact. A
blind man receiving sight, ever so imperfectly,
could never be ridiculed out of it, or argued out
of it, by the utmost shrewdness of his blind
companions. The glimpse of sunlight and trees
and flowers is enough for him ; and though he
cannot convince his blind companions by argument, he knows that he sees ; " light itself beareth
witness with the awakened light capacity within
him that he is a child of the daylight."

Recently there came under my ministerial
care a man of culture, education, refinement,
who had been restored to liberty after a period
of penal servitude. He told me that in his
youth he had been converted, the affirmation of
sonship had stirred within him, and that he had
never been able to silence its witness. He said
that when he began to wander from the path of
right he strove with the whole power of his
intellect to become an unbeliever ; that he came
to London and placed himself under the training
of Mr. Bradlaugh, in the eager desire to prove
his religion to be a lie ; but in vain. Out of the

lowest depths the Spirit ever bore tormenting
witness to him that he was a child of God. For
this is clearly one operation of the Spirit, which
equally bears witness to Divine sonship, but
which, inasmuch as it possesses an infinite
capacity for making men miserable, is constantly
misunderstood. It is the restless, galling sense
of self-conviction which stings the conscience
without comforting the heart. Men who are
perfectly conscious that they are under the
dark dominion of self-will wonder sometimes
why they are not happy in sensuality, why they
are wretched when they fall. The answer is :
" It is the witness within them of Divine sonship." It is the indwelling Spirit, the image of
God reflected in the soul of man, protesting,
perpetually and automatically, against being
smothered in unhallowed desires. It is the
standing tribunal of the Divine Logos, or Word,
immanent in all men, before which the doings
of the lower nature are perpetually brought for
judgment. If we were wholly animal or wholly
evil, we should not feel it. The fact that we
know that certain actions are wrong, even though
we continue to do them, is the absolute proof of
the existence within us of a moral judgment,
and a moral judgment is a proof of Divine sonship : the Spirit is bearing witness with our
spirit, that we are sons of God, though we are
dragging that sonship through the mire.

Finally, the teaching of the Gospel reveals the

method of our education, holds up an inspired mirror to ourselves, throws an electric searchlight upon the deepest problem of our nature. What is the spiritual meaning of this metaphor from the vegetable world about gathering grapes from thorns ? Obviously, the thorn and the thistle, the grape and the fig, cannot signify separate types of men, or the whole force of the metaphor would fail. The thorn and the thistle are obeying God's own law of heredity. and affinity by producing only thorns and thistles. They would violate the law of their being if they produced grapes and figs. No, it is just the old unvarying experience of the nature and constitution of man which perplexed and grieved St. Paul. It is an allegory of our separate selves, of that strange, complex nature of which we are so conscious, and which differentiates us from the lower animal. Each man is the soil in which the hereditary Adam seed produces thorn and thistle, and the hereditary God seed produces grape and fig ; the two growths in the same individual strive for the mastery, and from the deep contrast between them emerges the perfected life of the child of God. There is no other way, for thus hath the Father appointed. Salvation is character, not a scheme successfully to elude well-merited chastisement. There is no royal road to character ; " to him that overcometh " is the promise. The volition of the individual, stimulated by the breath of the Spirit of the Father, bearing witness to sonship, decides between the thorn nature and the vine nature almost every hour of every day. As God's sons we have the capacity, and we are given the responsibility, of living, by a definite effort and purpose, the higher life, the fruit-bearing life ; and, as we live it, we weaken and starve the thorn-bearing life. We are debtors, says the Apostle—we who know the secret of " Abba, Father "—not to the thorn and thistle, to live after the thorn and thistle ; for if we live after the thorn and thistle we must die ; but if we, through the Spirit, that is, through the development of the higher fruit-bearing nature, do mortify the deeds of the thorn and the thistle, we shall live.

Surely, this is the teaching of to-day. Every purposeful encouragement of Godward aspiration, every clinging to principle in time of temptation, every masterful conquest over sensual passion by ejaculatory prayer, every self-suppressing quenching of anger by the kind, gentle word, and every courageous witness against public wrong when self-interest would have kept us silent, ministers to the growth of the Divine fruit-bearing nature, and withers the thorn ; and, on the contrary, every conscious stifling of a good desire, every deliberate yielding to mere animalism, every refusal to recognize responsibility for the temptations of the weaker brother, every wilful violation of the everlasting distinction between right and wrong, blights and mildews the fruit-bearing nature, till the thorn and the thistle spring up and choke it. Thank God, the resources of His tireless love for every plant that the Heavenly Father hath planted are not exhausted, if the thorn and the thistle do thus choke the life, for there is the promise (which is a doom and a promise in one) that the thorn and the thistle shall be hewn down and cast into the fire ; but it will be a part of ourselves that will be thus burnt ; and this fire of remedial destruction is painted, in the parable of Dives, as of awfulness unspeakable. But we " have not received the spirit of bondage unto fear," but the Spirit of sonship, whereby we say, " Abba, Father."

Believe it ! intensely, practically, restfully. " If children, then heirs ; heirs of God, and joint heirs with Christ." Then, failing health, darkening prospects, the multitudinous sorrows of life, the puzzles of human education, will all be illuminated for us with the conviction that we are in God's infant school for the formation of character. As one says :

> I think that human lives
>   Must bear God's chisel keen,
> If the spirit yearns and strives
>   For the better life unseen.
> For men are only blocks at best,
> Till the chisel of God brings out the rest.

VIRTUE.

"Add to your faith virtue."—2 *Peter* i. 5.

THIS seems to be, according to St. Peter, the first step of the golden ladder by which man in his upward education arrives at the fully rounded Christian character. Before the foot is placed upon it, it is necessary to ascertain that the ladder is firmly based. The Revised Version supplies clearness to the injunction. The words are there rendered : " In your faith supply virtue."

" In your faith." The base of the ladder is a strong one. The pre-requisite condition of the ascent is important ; the assumption from which we commence to live the Christian life is far-reaching : " In your faith."

An almost universal misconception as to the nature of faith is responsible for much mental confusion between faith as a faculty in the nature of man, and believing, which is the faculty in operation. As sight is the faculty, and seeing is the faculty in operation, so faith is the faculty, and believing is the faculty in operation. The clearest definition of faith is in Hebrews xi.,

9

where it is described as a substance : " The
substance of things hoped for." Substance is a
word of recognized and emphatic meaning. Substance is the word used in the Nicene Creed for
the nature of God : " Of one substance with the
Father." Faith, then, is the Divine substance
in man ; it is the measure of the Divine life
that is in every man as his birthright ; it is the
universal sonship which in the Catholic Church
is solemnly claimed, ratified, and sealed for
each one in the sacrament of Holy Baptism.
When it is awakened, called into life, cultivated,
its outcome is believing, trusting, living, growing.
But it is there in every man, underlying all that
is most private and subtle even in secret thought.
It is a mirror which, when discovered, burnished,
and rightly adjusted, has the capability of reflecting so much as God reveals of Himself;
and when patiently turned Godward, its spiritual
discernment is quietly unfolded and it sees God
—sees Him as the one only power through all
puzzles and apparent contradictions, just as the
instinct of sonship in a child gradually sees the
love and care and purpose of a good father or
mother through the restraints and chastenings
and frets of childhood and boyhood.

The inward Divine substance called faith,
which is an attribute of our individuality,
reaching forth into the operation of believing,
trusting, and mastering difficulties, is similar in
its action to the operation of the Divine faculty

called intellect, which is an attribute of our personality, reaching forth into the acquisition of knowledge.

The mathematical master says to a boy at school, " Add to your intellect arithmetic "; or, " in your intellect supply arithmetic." Well, perhaps, when confronted with a difficult rule-of-three sum this boy dashes his book on the ground and stamps on it ; the result is that he becomes unmathematical. Many a man bidden to add to his faith " believing," or in his Divine substance to supply knowledge of God, at the first problem gives up and gets angry with the difficulties, and becomes an unbeliever, and for the rest of his life flaunts before the world the difficulties of the problem. Another boy looks on to the end of his arithmetic book, copies out the answer, and shows it up right ; his sum is correct, but he never learns arithmetic. How many similarly hand over the Divine faculty solidly to authority, either of an infallible book, or Church, or director, and remain quietly con-tent—*locuta est ecclesia controversio finita ?* they accept upon authority every creed in Christen-dom, but the science of God is unlearnt. A third boy, on the other hand, deliberately calls up his mental faculties to work out the sum in strict fidelity to certain known rules, and he brings the sum right ; he adds to his intelligence arithmetic, and to arithmetic algebra, and to algebra higher mathematics, till he gains the

mathematical tripos at Cambridge and is at the
top of his ladder. Similarly, a man who calls
upon the Divine substance within him, and
deliberately turns it Godward, and faces, from
this foundation, the difficult problems in God,
the world, and himself, slowly advances, rises
from strength to strength, from assurance to
assurance, the glass through which he sees
things becoming ever clearer and clearer, till
his trust in God and confidence in the Eternal
purpose is impregnable. He knows God, and
in that knowledge all things fall into place.

The first requisite, then, in considering St.
Peter's golden ladder of Christian acquirement
is the recognition of the fact that this substance
called faith, each man's measure of the Divine
life, the true individuality, is within us, and
that inasmuch as it is the germ of sonship, the
Christ nature in us, it has the power of unfolding,
and can do all things through the Christ that
strengtheneth it. Our assurance of this fact is
inextinguishable, as it is based on the revelation
of the Incarnation. The Divine Man outbreathed
into flesh, the perfect specimen of ideal manhood, is the pledge and guarantee of our own
sonship, for He has claimed us as brothers ;
He has said, " I go to My Father and to your
Father "; He has called Himself " the first-
born of many brethren," and has inspired an
Apostle to tell us that we are " God's heirs,
and joint heirs with Himself." The substance,

therefore, the Divine nature, the faith faculty, the true individuality, is there, and to this the Apostle appeals when he says, " In your faith supply virtue."

Consider it to-day. It is the Divine call to action ; it is God's protest against contented quietism, a dreary, contemplative mysticism ; it is the inspired trumpet call to exertion in the formation of character. The Apostle says : God hath endowed you with a Divine capacity, He has shared with you His mysterious Individuality ; unfold it, put it forth ; it can do all things through the Christ who will strengthen it ; it can cure you of vicious propensities ; it can remove mountains of appetite or habit, for it is " God that worketh in you." A nerveless, actionless, church-going, respectable assent is not faith. Be ashamed of your poor attainment, your idle life, your low standard, and to the sonship that God gave you add something you have wrought yourself—" add to your faith virtue."

It is an incontrovertible axiom that the only lifting power for the race, or for the individual, is action based on the confidence of the power to succeed ; or, in other words, in virtue added to faith. The truth is obvious in temporal matters. The cholera or the small-pox visit a community ; religious people begin to pray that the visitation may be removed. They cry to the Eternal as though He were inactive, or deaf, or asleep. Their faith is beyond all praise, but common sense and apostolic injunction both cry aloud, "Add to your faith virtue." Laws of sanitation have been grossly neglected, your water supply is defective, overcrowding and intemperance have been tolerated and encouraged ; the manual of devotion you need is not a prayer-book, but pure water, dust carts, and a few hundred shovels and brooms ; the incense you require is not the prayers of the saints, but chloride of lime and permanganate of potash. That was virtually the line that Palmerston took when he refused to order a day of public humiliation for the cholera, and in which he was vigorously supported by Kingsley.

Again, everyone remembers the well-worn tale of the pious lady of Vermont in the United States, the view from whose window was blocked by a rocky hill, and who determined to test the promise to faith that it should be removed and cast into the sea. And, according to her lights, she prayed and prayed the night through, till the dawn peeped in at the window, and there was the hill unmoved. " Ah ! " she said, " just as I expected ! " But there came along that way a prospecting engineer, with his instruments and chain measures and dumpy leveller, and examined that hill and accurately measured it. It was in the way of a new railroad, and he expressed his firm faith that it could be removed. The Company at his back adopted his faith, and

he added to his faith virtue in the shape of two
thousand navvies, and in a few months that
hill was removed. If he had had no faith, he
would not have put on the navvies; and if he
had not put on the navvies, his faith would have
been uninfluential and inactive. He added to
his faith virtue; he added to his orthodoxy
activity; he added to his creed conduct; he
added to his conviction action. His faith was
as the grain of mustard seed, which when the
life, or substance, is awakened within, moves
what, in comparison to its size, are literally
mountains. And so the engineer removed the
mountain that resisted the prayer, unmixed
with action, of the Christian lady of Vermont.

The conclusion is so obvious that application
is needless. To-day, to us, the Apostle says:
You have that grain of mustard seed, that
faith faculty which can remove mountains,
within you; add to that faith virtue. It is a
noble, expressive word. In Greek, *Arete*, from
Ares, the Greek name for Mars, the God of War;
in Latin, *virtus*, strength, from *vir*, a man. It
signifies manliness, and, in its special application, womanliness in the sense of womanly
chastity, brave and pure and strong, to with-
stand the selfish assaults of unmanly men.

A long list of heroes who added to their faith
virtue is provided in Hebrews xi.: Abel, Enoch,
Noah, Abraham, Joseph, Moses, and the vast
host of martyrs and confessors. These are the

aristocracy of grace. But there is a manliness,
not less heroic, within the reach of all. It is
easier in some great crisis, amidst the sympathy
and plaudits of thousands, to do noble deeds
for a holy cause, than quietly, patiently, unob-
trusively, in the monotony of the ever-recurring
cares of daily life, to live nobly, bravely for
Christ. This is manliness, virtue; this is the
experience in which many of God's heroes in
the poorest homes in London, and all the world
over, are adding to their faith virtue.

Brothers in God's school, it is well to watch
against the little unmanlinesses, the lesser meannesses that mar character and deteriorate
Christian life. Our lives are God-initiated, God-
inhabited, God-surrounded; for us Jesus lived
and died and survived; and it is in the lesser
details of daily discipline that He is building us
into men. Is it manly to be peevish and petulant and proud and sharp-tongued? Is it manly
to be courteous to strangers and rough and
ungentle at home? Is it manly to cower and
whimper and grumble under the educative discipline that meets us? Is it manly when you
have an anxiety to make everyone else bear it?
Is it manly to nurse that grudge, to repeat that
scandal, to envy that fellow man or fellow
woman? No, it is not manly, it is only mean;
and it is these lesser, unnoticed meannesses that
slowly deteriorate Christian character.

Lent is the time, the opportunity, to up and

sweep them away in the name of the Lord, and resolutely, determinedly, to " add to our faith virtue." Each Lenten season that does not stir us into action leaves the energies weaker, the desires more grovelling, the acquisition of virtue farther off.

" Awake, thou that sleepest." Power comes in doing ; resolutely to put sonship, faith, into operation constitutes a claim upon the power of our Divine Lord. To touch Him, if it is only the hem of His garment, is to draw virtue from Him into yourself. To touch Him ! Yes ! How ? By practice anywhere, anywhen, by momentary detachment, by ejaculation ; and, when this is difficult, mystically, spiritually, but intensely really, we can, we do touch Him in the faithful reception of the Holy Eucharist. I am, there-fore, justified in saying, " Ye that do truly and earnestly repent you of your sins, ye that intend to lead a new life " and to add to your faith virtue, draw near with that faith and take the Holy Sacrament to your comfort, and you will find the power you need to

" ADD TO YOUR FAITH VIRTUE."

KNOWLEDGE.

"Add to your virtue, knowledge."—2 *Peter* i. 5.

THERE are two ways of reading this inspired injunction : the one as it is translated in the Authorized Version, which is the version I have quoted ; the other as it is translated in the Revised Version. The distinction is interesting, as in the one case the injunction is subjective and in the other objective. Whichever translation you adopt, however, it teems with significance.

We will consider it first as it stands in the Authorized Version. On the natural, the material, the surface plane of thought it is a truism that needs no elaboration. Knowledge in every department of life is power. Virtue, in the sense of $\dot{a}\rho\epsilon\tau\dot{\eta}$, from Ares, the Greek name for Mars, Manliness, that which colloquially we call pluck, without knowledge is practically useless, excepting perhaps to a bulldog. The man who knows is always a head and shoulders above the man who does not know, though the latter may be the superior of the former in vigour and endurance. What is the justification for the

millions we spend annually in secular education ?
It is that ignorance is the mother of degradation ;
knowledge is the road to moral and social improvement. Plato says : " Better be unborn
than untaught, for ignorance is the root of mis-
fortune." From knowledge comes industry, for
knowledge knows how little it knows, and longs
and hungers to know more. How deep is the
debt that human society owes to the industry
of the knowledge-hunters ; from the laborious
researches which have revealed the elemental
laws written all over this radiant universe on
rock, and grass-blade, and the structure of plants
and animals. From how many superstitions have
they freed us ! from how dense a materialism
have they led us forth ! They have made the
world luminous by discovering in it an order
of rational thought, and they have caused the
animal and vegetable kingdoms to teem with
suggestions of the Infinite. These physical investigators have added to their virtue, knowledge ; and as they pass to a higher life, which
perhaps they have not here acknowledged, they
leave the world better than they found it. So,
irrespective of the deeper destinies of the human
race, if you would love life and see good days,
and help others, " add to your virtue, knowledge."

St. Peter does not suggest the method ; St.
Paul does. " Give attention to reading," he
says to Timothy ; and he was right, for reading

makes the full man ; it fills him with facts of
physiology, facts of history, facts of mathematics. And the conquest of any one truth
on any subject-matter has a moral value : it
not only adds to the treasures of the memory,
increases the force of the intelligence, ennobles
the conception of the universe, but it distinctly
braces and invigorates the will. So the prudent
man will obey the injunction of St. Peter and
perpetually enlarge his sphere of information ;
he will realize that his education is never complete. Like Michael Angelo, who at a great age
was found studying the architecture of the
Coliseum, and muttering, " The old man goes
yet to school," he will be ever eager to learn
something new, and will recognize that for the
mind of man the only " finishing tutor," so to
speak, is death.

It is, however, certain that the Apostle is
leading us into deeper waters than these. "Add
to your virtue, knowledge " is a challenge to
the profoundest instinct in the human heart ;
an instinct which, if it be not an affirmation of
God and immortality, is wholly inexplicable ;
a yearning after the Unseen, a tentative intuition,
an upward thinking that has been a characteristic of mankind always and everywhere. Plato
calls it " the upward attraction of the soul ";
Aristotle calls it " the universal hypothesis of
the unseen "; Epicurus calls it " the world-wide
prejudice of the Divine "; Cicero calls it " the

anticipation naturally embedded in the human mind "; St. Paul calls it " the Christ in you, the hope of glory." Whatever you call it, it is a fact in human psychology ; it is " God-hunger," the capacity for the Divine, the hereditary spark from the universal Parent. You cannot define it. It has been named the intuitive, as distinct from the rational faculty ; but it eludes you if you strive to put it into words. When you can express harmony by the laws of logic, you can perhaps crystallize into a proposition that ray of Divine light in the heart of man which, when kindled, enables him to see through the earthly into the heavenly, through the apparent into the real, through the shadow into the substance, and to feel assured that somehow and some-when he came out from the Father and came into the world, and that somewhen and some-how he will leave the world and go to the Father.

Now, St. Peter says, call this into activity. With watchful, prayerful culture it will grow; it will expand and strengthen with every de-liberate use, with every earnest prayer, true intercession, believing communion ; it will be dimmed and clouded by whatever sensualizes and materializes the life. So " add to your manliness, God knowledge." As thou wouldest train thyself for a literary, scientific, or com-mercial life, so train thyself for a life towards God, which is Eternal Life ; for " this is life Eternal, to know Thee the only God and Jesus Christ whom Thou hast sent."

Why does this injunction glide languidly over unroused consciences ? Partly from sheer indolence ; partly from a deeper reason, a casuistic reason. If it were expressed, it would take this shape : " I do not desire to know more about God ; furnish me with a working philosophical explanation of the universe, some creeds and dogmas with traditional sanction, and certain authoritative rules of right and wrong, and I am content. Greater knowledge implies greater responsibilities. The imperfection of man's knowledge is the measure of man's innocence ; keep a man ignorant and you keep him innocent." J. J. Rousseau carried this theory into the realm of material life, and urged that men should live without education that they might be saved from the miseries and vices which cling around the steps of advancing civilization. The answer is that this attitude contradicts the universal law of growth and development ; it contradicts the Divine method of the evolution, whether of a plant or of a human soul. Whatever the risk, whatever the increase of responsibility, whatever the new possibilities of evil, knowledge must be acquired that the end may be attained.

What an illustration we have in the story of the Fall. The pastoral idyll of the Garden of Eden is an allegory of this law, which, inasmuch as it is universal and eternal, must be Divine. The so-called Fall of Man was the direct result of obedience, by anticipation, to the inspired injunction of the Apostle Peter to " add to vigorous humanity, knowledge."

If emancipated from the letter and awake to the spiritual inwardness, you recognize one of God's majestic disclosures. The particular form in which this story is recorded was obviously assumed after the return of the Jews from the Babylonish captivity. Their Jehovah worship was leavened with a misunderstood Zoroastrianism ; the serpent is manifestly the counterpart of the Ahriman of Zoroastrianism, and that mythical personage was afterwards developed into the conception of Satan. But Ahriman was something wholly different from the Satan conception—Ahriman was a kind of petulant mischief-maker, a sort of Puck, whose function it was to mar the handiwork of Ormuzd, the Spirit of Good, his twin brother, but who in his freaks of mischief unwittingly fulfilled the deep-hidden purpose of the Absolute Will and so promoted, instead of hindering, the education of the human race.

It was so here. Though the serpent intended mischief, he spoke a profound truth : " Ye shall become as gods, knowing good and evil." According to the story in Genesis, this was the testimony of God Himself : " Behold the man has become as one of us " (as one of the Elohim), " to know good and evil." True, man inherited the curse which, like all God's curses, was a blessing in disguise; the curse-blessing which abolishes the demoralization of a life without labour, the unprogressive, non-moral condition of untempted innocence, introducing the secret of happiness which is the dignity of labour; and the possibility of perfection, which is the steady rising on the "stepping stones of the dead self to higher things."

We may, for purposes of rudimentary exposition, theologically call it the Fall, but metaphysically it was the first step in the long upward education of a moral being, and this first step was the acquisition of knowledge. It was as necessary for man to descend into the material to become a moral being as it is necessary for an acorn to be buried in the earth to become an oak. And though the whole history is cast into the form of a picturesque oriental allegory with a Persian colouring, and though St. Paul uses the story to emphasize his teaching that the Christ was the second Adam—that is, that He represented the divine aspect of the race as Adam represented the human—it is clear that he perceived that the Eternal could never have been outwitted or taken by surprize, for he emphatically declares in Rom. viii. that the creature (that is, man) was made subject to vanity (that is, led into what theologically is called the Fall); not willingly, but by reason of Him (that is, God); and though the consequences are groaning and travailing now, the "whole creation shall be delivered from the bondage of corruption into the glorious liberty of the children of God ;" but only by the steady, gradual, continuous conquest of the lower life by the higher, by the coming into the soul, and out from the soul, more and ever more of the pure and noble Eternal life, which is the increasing knowledge of God ; by working out your own salvation, which is calling into activity the Divine germ of salvation within you, as an acorn works out its own oak tree perfection by the development of the germ infolded in its nature. So add ceaselessly to your humanity, knowledge of God. Each fresh knowledge will cause unrest in your carnal soul ; there will be sighing, and sobbing, and sadness, and anxiety, and the turning out from many an Eden of quiet self-indulgence, as the contrast between what you are, and what you now see you ought to be, becomes more manifest to you. But in this condition of conflict and unrest you will read God's promise of a higher, nobler manhood, and find the stimulus for a more earnest development of your ideal humanity.

It is exactly by such unrest that the pursuit of knowledge is stimulated on the material plane. It is just because man is " made subject to vanity " that he is stimulated to the struggle against it. Discomfort, pain, inability, limitation, catastrophe—all these lead to investigation of causes, reflection, effort, invention, discovery, and ultimate in knowledge—physical, mental, mechanical—the influence of which in the increased happiness of mankind is incalculable. The natural is the shadow of the spiritual, it is not otherwise in spiritual things. Mrs. Browning says :

> Glory to God, glory to God,
> Knowledge by suffering entereth,
> And life is perfected by death.

So let our infirm, temptable, suffering humanity drive us only deeper into the knowledge of God as we " add to virtue, knowledge."

I will not attempt to define this increasing knowledge, it is too interior and profound ; but it is accustoming yourself to the thought that one Infinite life is everywhere present, that God and man are inseverable, that Jesus Christ is the Sacrament of God, that the inmost life of everyone is hid with Christ in God, that sin is a profanation of His temple, and that salvation is not an expedient or a scheme, but character built up by the evolution of the " Christ in you, the hope of glory."

It would be easy to show by countless examples that the grandest characters amongst the sons of men are ever those in which knowledge has been thus added to virtue ; in which great intellectual power, or conspicuous physical prowess have been softened, sanctified, and elevated by individual intercourse with God. Such men as examples of physical prowess were Havelock,

Hedley Vicars, Gordon, Lord Airlie who was shot at Diamond Hill. The army has produced and is producing scores of such men. Again, in the sphere of intellectual distinction we think of Galileo, Agassiz, Newton, W. B. Carpenter, and many other intellectual giants ; they added to their acquired prowess, or to their vast fund of natural facts, the knowledge of God, and they have each and all, in their measure, earned the reverence and the love of their fellow men, and the world is the better that they have lived.

The injunction is as powerful and as influential when considered in the translation of the Revised Version : " In your manliness supply knowledge "; in other words, " Impart your knowledge with unflinching courage." No man can be a genuine helper of humanity if from timidity, from desire of personal ease, from dread of disturbing traditional opinions, he stifles within him knowledge which would benefit the race and which is striving for utterance. Great causes have been blighted, the upward evolution of the race has been hindered, when men in positions of authority and influence have feared " in their manliness to supply knowledge." They have seen their nation steeped in suffering and in sin, they have watched the monstrous growth of public evil, their hearts have burned within them, they have felt the strivings of the instinct of reform, but they have lacked the manliness to shock conventionality, to startle unbroken

tradition, to irritate long-closed eyelids, and
they have remained timidly silent; the world is
not the better that such men lived. Not thus
was John the Baptist in the palace of Herod ;
not thus was Latimer at the Court of Henry
VIII. ; not thus was Charles Kingsley at the
time of the Chartist agitation ; not thus was
Lord Shaftesbury when he fought the battle of
the children in the mines and the chimneys.

With what peculiar emphasis, moreover, does
this injunction of St. Peter apply to the wider
horizons of truth that, under the teaching of
God's Spirit, are opening everywhere in this age
around theological thought. Some ray of clearer
light pours through the mist of imperfect apprehension of the nature and character of God
and of the universality of redemption. This is
not surprizing. Christ told us that it would be
so. He declared that the twilight should brighten
more and more, that the full truth should break
gradually upon the intelligence of the world.
It has not all shone forth yet ; the sun is still
rising. But meanwhile the twilight has become
crystallized into conventional beliefs. These conventional beliefs are made the shibboleths of
certain religious schools of thought. If in your
manliness you begin to supply knowledge, to
become a transmitter of this light you have seen ;
if you suggest that identification is a higher word
than propitiation, that Father is a truer name
than God, you grieve, you anger, you irritate.

The line of least resistance, especially to a teacher, is to hold your peace ; quietly, " after the way that they call heresy," to worship the God of your fathers ; but Nicodemus-like, and by night, for fear of the orthodox.

My fellow-students in the knowledge of the Eternal, " in your manliness supply knowledge " as opportunity offers. Help by your testimony to vindicate that higher knowledge of God which in consideration for human weakness He seems to have withheld in earlier revelation, but with which the Spirit is in these days flooding the Churches.

> I say to thee, do thou repeat
> To the first man thou mayest meet
> In lane, highway, or open street,
> That he, and we, and all men move
> Under a canopy of Love
> As broad as the blue sky above ;
> That we, on divers shores now cast,
> Shall meet, our perilous voyage past,
> All in our Father's home at last.

Amen. Verily, it is so. God help us thus " in our virtue to supply knowledge."

SELF-CONTROL.

"Add to your knowledge, self-control."—2 *Peter* i. 6.

AGAIN there is to be noted a distinction between the injunction as it appears in the
Authorized Version and as it appears in the
Revised Version. If time permits, I should like
to consider both. First, as it is recorded in the
Authorized Version, it is an appeal to the germ
of our ideal humanity. I have retranslated one
word only. The word " temperance," since the
date of the Authorized Version, has grown into
a more exclusive use, which cramps its true
signification. The Greek word 'εγκράτεια classically
means self-control, self-mastery, and is so used
frequently by Plato and by Aristotle. Now,
what is 'εγκράτεια, " self-control " ? I do not
mean in the separate details of its normal application ; these will differ in different tempera-
ments ; but what is it in its principle, its essence ?
In its deepest, truest signification it can only
follow knowledge, such knowledge as that of
which I spoke in the previous sermon ; that
awakened and illuminated perception that enables a man to see a little, just a little, through

the earthly into the heavenly, through the apparent into the real, through the shadow into the substance, and to feel, perhaps dimly, but with ever-increasing assurance, that in this universe one Infinite life is everywhere present ; that from the unthinkable centre to the utmost boundary of being one law is ruling, one love is pulsing, and that all creatures live and move and have their being in God. It is no discredit to the earnest, loving souls of the past to say that this knowledge is a comparatively late revelation. It was the want of this knowledge, or the refusal to receive this knowledge, that originated the narrow, self-torturing conception of self-control of the Latin theologians ; that placed St. Simon Stylites on his pillar ; that prompted the Abbe de Rancé to found the Order of La Trappe ; that induced the celebrated Madame Guyon, at the beginning of the seventeenth century, to mix her food with wormwood, to have sound teeth extracted as a conciliation of God, and to drop burning sealing-wax on her fingers for the same purpose.

It was this limited conception of God as the objective, irresponsible, implacable despot outside the universe, and the complete ignorance of God as the Universal, Responsible, Immanent Parent Source whence all forms of individual existence emerge, that originated the accursed cruelties of the Inquisition, and the conviction that self-control implied the duty to scourge,

root out, annihilate all that was natural, material, temporal. The "new theology," which I
prefer to call the reversion to the pure theology
of Clement of Alexandria and Athanasius, the
theology which is "sweeping the cobwebs all
away from Jesus Christ, the door," teaches a
deeper, fuller doctrine of self-control.

What, then, is self-control from the deeper,
the more esoteric point of view ? To answer
the question I must turn from St. Peter to St.
Paul. St. Peter would probably have excelled
St. Paul in catching fish and in estimating their
market value when caught. St. Paul would have
excelled St. Peter in weaving the meshes of the
net of metaphysics, and in recognizing the life-
sustaining power of which the fish was an expression. They had been differently educated,
and had different minds.

St. Paul, in speaking of self-control, says :
" I keep under my body." Again, in the Epistle
to the Ephesians, he speaks of " the power that
worketh in you." It is evident that he knew
the mystery of man. Man, the puzzle of the
ages, the riddle of the Sphinx, the problem of
the metaphysician, the despair of the biologist,
man is a complex being, combining within him
elements apparently opposite in moral tendency.
In Scripture these elements are called " flesh
and spirit." The one is the animal nature, the
vital centre and seat of the personal existence,
wherein are subjectively realized animal wants,

appetites, feelings, impulses ; the other is the spiritual nature, the centre and realm of all the higher endowments and potentialities of spiritual manhood. The one, the animal, has a tendency, when unregulated, to sensualize, vulgarize, brutalize ; the other, when developed, has a tendency to refine, to purify, to ennoble. At first sight these elements appear to be unfairly balanced, for the animal nature is the first to awaken, the fleshly drawing is in full force before the moral faculty has come into conscious activity ; so the fleshly desires get, as it were, the start. But when the spiritual nature is awake, though last in order of time, it becomes first in order of authority ; the appetites which, under the limitations of inexperience and the imperfections of scarcely-awakened moral consciousness, have exercised undisputed sway, find that they are in the presence of a rival who means to be master, to whose rule and influence they must finally surrender. Why ? Because this higher nature in man is not (as some have profanely taught) a collection of religious prejudices instilled in childhood, but the Divine nature in man. It is God manifest in flesh. It is Divine love moving in man in a mystery of wisdom. This is the " God-self " as contrasted with the nature-self ; its promptings are the echo of God's voice in the soul. When St. Paul called it " the Christ in you the hope of glory," he proclaimed the grand Athanasian teaching that

God's full Christ is not one man, but the whole
multitudinous race-life in Him ; that God's
life in man is man's eternal hope ; and that this
higher life effects the perfection of poor humanity
not by cauterizing and tormenting and extirpating the animal nature, but by absorbing,
transmuting, transfiguring, at-one-ing it to the
Divine. Thus self-control is not, as it were,
the natural self in civil war ; it is the God-self
regulating and controlling the nature-self ; and
the growth of character is from within outwards,
and not from without inwards—not as revolution, but as evolution. The religious life is not a
system of mortifications, but a growth. Purer
morals, wider creeds, higher ideals, nobler standards are evolved from a Divine secret within,
as fruit is evolved on a tree. The well-known
horticultural process of grafting affords an illustration. What does a skilful gardener do with
a hedge briar ? He can never make it into a
rose by mortifying it or cauterizing it or annihilating it. He takes it from the hedge, plants
it in the garden, and grafts on to it the choice
rose. The result is not two hostile identities,
but one life ; two natures making one individuality, but the original individuality only
allowed to express itself through the new and
imparted nature. The rose has become the new
life, and all the natural vigour and energy of the
hedge briar contributes to the life of the rose.
The awakening of the Divine consciousness in

man is the grafting into the animal nature of
the new life of sonship. The old life is hid in the
new life, all its energy and vitality are to be
transformed and utilized and made to contribute
to the development of the new life. So, self-
control is in reality not negative, but positive ;
it is not the condemning, crushing, extirpating all
the tendencies of the nature-life, but the watchful, prayerful culture of the Divine life within.
That which overcomes the qualities and limitations of the nature-life within us is the strong,
purposeful affirmation of the indwelling of God's
universal Spirit. I am not, of course, speaking
as though I had attained, but I am indicating
an ideal that I can see is undeniably true when
I say that if when a man felt the strong solicita-
tion of the lower nature, the tendency to be
angry, selfish, untruthful, unchaste, he were
able instantly to focus his mental faculties upon
the transcendent truth that God's life, God's
Spirit, dwelt in him, that the fruit of God's
Spirit is love, peace, purity, self-control ; if
with a resolute Godward uplifting of his inmost
he, in the moment of temptation, claimed the
co-operation of the " power that worketh in
him," the result would be an instant subduing
of those lower impulses for that time ; and as
each conquest of the lower life by the higher
means an increase of the pure and noble life of
sonship, every conquest in temptation would be
a strengthening of the true ego, an onward step

towards that consummation of pure self-control,
when he will be able to say with St. Paul, " I
keep under my body;" the divinity that stirs
within me now controls and dominates the
humanity in which I am embodied. The so-
called Christian Scientists of our day are using
this very principle of the affirmation of the
God-self for the cure of the diseases of the body,
and not without success, and it is certainly
the cure for diseases of the moral nature. There
is a remarkable letter from Southey to Charlotte
Brontë in which he says : " It is by God's mercy
in our power to attain a degree of self-government
which is essential to our happiness and contributes greatly to that of those around us—
keep a quiet mind for your health's sake. Your
moral and spiritual improvement will then keep
pace with the cultivation of your intellectual
power." In other words, he said to her, " Add
to your knowledge, self-control."

" In your knowledge, supply self-control."
The solemn duty of supplying knowledge with
manliness, of constantly speaking the truth
and boldly rebuking vice, must be tempered by
a watchful prudence and self-restraint. In knowledge of God, to allow your courageous declaration of a Divine truth to outrun your real conviction, or your serious purpose, or your just
opportunity ; in social reform, to cast out
demons through Beelzebub, the prince of the
demons, or, in other words, to overcome evil

with evil, as anarchists would overcome social wrong with dynamite ; in family life or in friendship, to tell out to another an unpleasant truth in a cynical, unloving, fault-finding spirit ; this it is to supply knowledge without self-control, and neither to serve humanity nor to obey God. The first characteristic of self-control in supplying knowledge is humility ; it is ever the best informed that utter knowledge most humbly and tentatively, who say " This is what I see, this is true to myself "; it is ever the shallowest who utter their knowledge with the most dogmatic self-conceit. As real knowledge, the inner spiritual knowledge of God, increases, self-depreciation and self-control increase also.

A lesson might well be learnt from the designations of the students in the ancient Greek University of Athens. Their first designation was Sophoi, or the wise. After a year's residence they rose to the title of Philosophoi, or the lovers of wisdom ; and finally, when their course of instruction was complete, they were designated Mathetai, or disciples. Every increase of knowledge, you observe, was estimated as a demonstration of the vast treasures of knowledge as yet unknown, and was expected to bring with it increasing humility and self-depreciation. Is it not thus when " the minds of men are widening with the process of the suns," and widening Godwards ? As the mind unmoors from narrow conceptions and draws nearer to

the great ocean of uncreated light, which is God
Himself, dogmatism becomes impossible, the
Sophoi become Mathetai, the mental attitude is,
" Lead, kindly Light, lead Thou me on ; So far
Thy power hath led me, sure it still will lead me
on."

I know I have only touched the borders of
this theme, but I would rather leave each one
to bring down the injunction into the details of
daily life for himself, only emphasizing that the
knowledge of one's own utter ignorance and
unworthiness is the surest counterpoise to any
risk of lack of self-control in supplying knowledge with manliness in every relation of life.
There are in Scripture many examples of occasions when " speech may be silvern, but silence
is golden." When, for instance, to supply knowledge would be manifestly useless ; when, as our
Lord says, it would be casting pearls before
swine ; silence is then golden. Or when it would
be obviously harmful, as in the ready-tongued
repetition of some rumour to the discredit of
another. " Thou shalt not," said Jehovah, " go
up and down as a tale-bearer among my people."
Or when it is in praise of yourself. " Let another
praise Thee," said the author of the Book of
Proverbs, " and not thine own mouth." Or
when the knowledge is not your own to supply,
as when the servant of Midas could not control
himself from whispering his master's secret to
the rushes ; or when the knowledge can only

cause jealousy and dissension, as when Joseph, as recorded in this morning's first lesson, could not keep his dreams to himself.

The whole teaching of this, and, indeed, of every aspect of the text, is summed up in the historic scene of the world's representative Man, the Word Incarnate, before the judgment seat of Pilate. It is the supreme, the transcendent exhibition of " self-control added to knowledge." As the Eternal Reason of God embodied, He was the Incarnation of all knowledge ; one out-flash of His knowledge would have changed the judgment seat into a throne, but it would have hindered the Divine purpose, for it would have established the Kingdom of Heaven upon earth, and so He who " spake as no man ever spake " was in that crisis silent, as no man was ever silent. He stood in their midst calm, majestic, fearless, but silent. And so long as the world lasteth that silence of Jesus rebukes human impatience, human irritability, human self-glorification, and proclaims this injunction of St. Peter :

" IN YOUR KNOWLEDGE SUPPLY SELF-CONTROL."

PATIENCE.

" Add to your self-control, patience."—2 *Peter* i. 6.

THE fact that this word occurs so late in the list of the steps of ethical attainment according to St. Peter, after faith and virtue and knowledge and self-control, suggests that in its deepest signification it is a quality appertaining only to an advanced stage of spiritual acquirement. Possibly that is why I find myself only able to look upon it from afar, and feel that I am more likely to give you occasion in this sermon to exercise the virtue of patience than to contribute enlightenment as to its nature. I cannot define it except by emphasizing our bitter experience of its opposite, and I fear I know more of impatience than of patience, though I have to preach upon patience. Shakespeare says: " 'Tis all men's office to preach patience to those who writhe under the load of scorn, but no man's moral when he shall endure the like himself." Looking upon this virtue from the modest distance of a pupil, I can see that patience is a passive, not an active virtue. It is a certain interior disposition or attitude of the soul which human beings rarely acquire save in the school of suffering ; people are rarely patient by nature. When they appear to be, it is often a constitutional amiability—a functional quietism—a lymphatic indolence, rather than true patience. True patience is learnt in the school of suffering, and I have often been rebuked, stimulated, and taught by the unmurmuring patience I have seen exercised in the homes of the poor.

The Greek word, ὑπομονή, here translated patience, means, etymologically, rather the school in which patience is learnt than actual patience. Ὑπομονή, classically, means remaining behind, either taking or being forced to take the hindermost place, being compelled to stand still when you desire to go forward ; and no discipline can be imagined more severe for the average restless human character. Experience, however, is constantly proving that this ὑπομονή is a condition, an ingredient of real progress. For example, during that black week when we were all horror-stricken at our early reverses in South Africa, an experienced soldier assured me that these reverses would prove to be the salvation of the situation. If, he said, a few flashy successes had attended our arms at the first, we should have failed to recognize the seriousness of the undertaking. No reinforcements would have been prepared, transports and remounts would not have been forthcoming, and when our forces had penetrated into the country far from

their base, our well-armed, mobile, and perfectly
prepared enemy would have surrounded us,
and great disaster would have followed. I think
he was right. The ὑπομονὴ, the setting back,
stirred the nation to its depths, penetrated to
its true resources, manifested the reality of
Imperial unity, transfigured noisy self-idolatry
into real patriotism, elevating and invigorating
the whole national character. This ὑπομονὴ, then,
is rather the school of patience than patience
itself, and the man who has reached the step in
St. Peter's category called self-control, has
matriculated into the school where in time he
will learn patience. We have all known such
men in all departments of human activity : in
art, and science, and literature, and philanthropy.
We have wondered at the complete absence of
any eagerness for immediate results, of any
propensity for judging effort by rapid and showy
effects. They have seemed to be sustained by
a quiet assurance that labour on correct principles must issue in success. Lord Kitchener's
railway to Khartoum is a conspicuous example
of the result of this attitude of mind. Dis-
couraged by every engineer he consulted, baffled
by floods and sandstorms, opposed at every step
by hostile bands of Dervishes, he persevered.
The strength and secret of his success was that
he added to his self-control, patience. It is
the same in the plane of scientific achievement.
Kepler, who discovered the wondrous laws of

the wheeling planets, was met with contempt,
irritation, incredulity by his contemporaries. He
died poor, neglected, despised. On his deathbed
a friend condoled with him that he was un-
appreciated. " My friend," he said, " God has
waited thousands of years for one of His sons
to discover the admirable laws by which He
governs the stars. Cannot I wait also till justice is done to me ?" He had added to his
knowledge, self-control, and to his self-control,
patience. Such patience is heaven's inexhaustible antidote to at least half of the thousand
and one ills that flesh is heir to. It is " too
wonderful and excellent for me, I cannot attain
to it," but I can see that it is to have a guardian
angel ever near you, shielding you from the
fiery darts. So, obviously, thought Whittier
when he wrote those lovely lines :

> Angel of Patience ! sent to calm
> Our feverish brows with cooling palm—
> To lay the storms of hope and fear,
> And reconcile life's smile and tear ;
> The throbs of wounded pride to still,
> And make our own our Father's will.
>
> He walks with thee, that angel kind,
> And gently whispers—be resigned ;
> Bear up, bear on, the end shall tell
> The dear Lord ordereth all things well.

Now, if I am concerned to endeavour to obey
the injunction of St. Peter, and, in the words of
Milton, " arm my breast with stubborn patience
as with triple steel," it is well to ascertain the

11—2

conditions in the ordinary discipline of human
life in which we are most liable to impatience.
They are, of course, multitudinous; but in the
experience of most of us there are three degrees
of impatience : impatience with our fellow men ;
impatience with ourselves ; impatience with God.
And, first, impatience with our fellow men. It
is a sad fact that half the sanctifying power of
life is lost by our impatience with others. And
yet the Christian ideal contemplates each heart
as having interdependencies with its fellows,
and holds each one answerable for his influence
on every life of those around him. I pass by,
as too obvious to need emphasizing, the fre-
quency with which we positively kill spiritual
influence by exhibitions of impatience in ordinary home life—in the relations between husband and wife, parent and child, master and
servant, teacher and pupil. " God, God forgive
us all." Most of us are terribly impatient with
children, and yet that is worst of all impatience.
Dean Stanley, in his life of Arnold, relates how
Dr. Arnold told him that in his early days as
a schoolmaster he lost patience with a dull boy.
The lad looked up in his face, and said : " Why
do you speak angrily, sir ; indeed, I am doing
the best I can." Dr. Arnold said : " I never
was so ashamed in my life ; that look and that
speech cured me, and I don't think I was ever
impatient with a dull boy again."

Consider, again, how impatient, how intolerant

we are with the religious opinions and practices
of others. Calvin said : " I have not nearly so
great a struggle with my vices as I have with
my impatience. I have never been able to tame
this wild beast." Well, I confess, I am equally
impatient with the hideous theology of Calvin.
And all such impatience is utterly irrational,
it is the blight and shame of modern Christendom.
The Emperor Charles V. tried, by violent
measures, to make twenty millions of people
agree in their religious opinions. He realized
his folly when, in after life, he retired to a monas-
tery and amused himself by constructing clocks,
and found by repeated experiments that, with
all his skill, he was unable to make two clocks
go exactly alike for any length of time. Impatience with another man's religious conceptions
is practically denial of an everlasting fact. Unity
is not a successful scheme for theological same-
ness and ritual uniformity, but a keener realization of the universal immanence of the Spirit
of God, which immanence will find outward expression in many different ways. Strive to
amalgamate a heap of steel filings, and you will
strive in vain ; plunge a magnet into them,
and it will be covered with adhering atoms,
and the gathered atoms will attract others by
a force, secret, inexplicable, invisible. It is a
parable of the future of the Churches, when the
doctrine of essential Fatherhood as the ground
of universal existence has been plunged deep

into the, at present, disintegrated atoms, and the conception of God as the one universal indwelling Spirit has become generally accepted in the religious world and has welded together hearts now sundered by distinctions of creed, method, and sect; until which time, considering that affirmations that seem like contradictions are not only often true together, but are together necessary to express the full truth, the wise man will add to his self-control, patience.

Then how impatient we often are with other men's indifference to measures of social reform in which we are interested. I do not speak of politics : men are notoriously impatient with other men's political opinions. But this sentence of St. Peter might almost have been written for those of us who have been fighting for many years against the open cancer of our national life—the vice of intemperance. " Add to your temperance, self-control ; and to your self-control, patience," might well be the motto of the temperance reformer. Religious people will continue to look on with cold indifference while you wrestle and strive ; human perversity will continue to render ineffective every effort for the moral reformation of the nation ; the concocters of shallow epigrams will continue to feed with their thin, paltry sophisms the flame which is consuming the masses. So St. Peter says : " Add to your temperance, patience." Not, of course, with the preventible causes of your nation's sin—there can be no armistice with them ; but with the dull perversity of your brother Christian, and with the slow process of moral regeneration, which, inasmuch as it is part of the evolution of the Divine Spirit, can never ultimately be defeated. Again, why are we so impatient with our fellow man when he misrepresents us, and slanders us, and filches our good name ? It would be sufficient to fall back on Cowper's epigram, and say : " The modest, the sensible, the well-bred man will not insult me, and *none other can.*" One of our Bishops, when he was a London incumbent, was at one time deeply distressed by the persistent calumnies of a certain obnoxious parishioner. He wrote for advice to a high legal luminary, who was also a very religious man (once a Sunday school teacher, by the way, in St. John's School). His answer was laconic ; it was a quotation : " ' Jesus stood before the governor, and when He was accused of the chief priests and elders, He answered nothing, insomuch that the governor marvelled greatly.' Dear so-and-so, let the governor marvel greatly." Let that thought challenge us when next we are smarting impatiently under an unjust accusation. Let the silence of Jesus, the transcendent embodiment of perfect patience, teach us to add to our self-control, patience.

We are also impatient with ourselves, with our feeble attainment, our halting progress, our many mistakes, our frequent falls. This, too, is irrational. No strong Christian character was ever built up quickly. Christian character is not a transformation scene, it is a growth ; a slow, gradual unfolding of a principle of interior vitality. All true growth places a strain on patience. Some of us have seen the mango trick in India ; that is not how God grows a mango, or a Christian soul. A violinist once asked Paganini how long it would take him to learn to play as well as the master. " O ! twelve hours a day for twenty years," was the reply. You confound the whole philosophy of your being when you think to attain goodness by short cuts. Keep the inmost, the life secret whence action and emotion spring, open towards God in prayer, communion, soul out-pouring, and the diviner practice slowly, slowly, but none the less surely, comes ; and be not impatient that the mills of God grind slowly. John Wesley, in his seventy-third year, wrote : " I feel, I grieve, but by the grace of God I fret at nothing." He had added to his self-control, patience.

Finally. Patience must reach into the purpose of the ages ; we must be patient with God. It is no use denying that our Heavenly Father often puts a strain upon our patience. The problem of pain, the mystery of iniquity, the malignity of animal passions, the prevalence of moral evil, the sufferings of children and of irresponsible living creatures, afford matter for persevering, anxious, weary thought, and tend to impatience, to the reiterated cry : " How long, O Lord ?" But God is the Responsible

Creative Spirit, whose resources are unlimited and whose omnipotence and rectitude are at stake in perfecting the creation which is an expression of Himself. " He is patient," says Augustine, " because He is everlasting." With patience He will win the souls of men, with patience He will liquidate the debt that He owes to creation. " Have patience with Me," says God, " and I will pay thee all." With patience, says the Persian proverb, the mulberry leaf becomes satin. With patience, God's patience, shall the infinite confusion of the conditioned state become final order in the unerring, unfailing purpose of God. Be patient, therefore, with God. Rest in the Lord and wait patiently for Him. Patience with God is conscious self-surrender to the Eternal purpose; it is a gentle, tender, mighty trust ; it is a quenchless assurance, an inextinguishable conviction, that the Infinite and Universal Parent Spirit has begotten His own nature in us, and that we, and our dearest ones, and all men, are safe in His Almighty care. " My Father," said Jesus, " is greater than all, and no man can snatch out of My Father's hand." It is the attitude so beautifully expressed by Adelaide Procter :

I do not ask, O Lord, that Thou should'st shed full radiance
    here,
Give but a ray of peace, that I may tread without a fear ;
I do not ask my cross to understand, my way to see,
Better in darkness just to feel Thy hand and follow Thee.
Joy is like a restless day, but peace Divine like quiet night.
Lead me, O Lord, till perfect day shall shine through peace
    to light.

GODLINESS.

" Add to your patience godliness."—2 *Peter* i 6.

HOW can I venture to speak of godliness ?
I can imagine that some who may have
followed my thoughts, as together we have
climbed this ladder of ethical attainment provided by St. Peter, will have come to this same
conclusion, namely, that to-day, at any rate,
I have arrived at an insurmountable barrier. I,
like you, am a learner, trying to devote myself
to the training of the soul's power. And though
godliness is a transcendent ideal far beyond my
power of attainment, I will be of good cheer,
because I know that God's life in man is the
secret of man's eternal progress, and that the
Infinite Love and Reason is ever striving to
unfold itself in each one of us. One thing is
clear, godliness is both the test and the outcome
of patience ; and man's mental, moral, and
affectional nature will never be capable of truly
knowing and reflecting God till it has been
trained in the school of patience : that patience
which means so much more than quelling irritability ; that patience which reaches out into the

purpose of the ages, which includes immovable
confidence in the limitless resources of the everlasting Father of Spirits, unshakable assurance
in His will and power to bring at last all
creaturely life into complete harmony with His
perfect, universal will ; that patience which
trusts God wholly ; that patience which will
bear the test of adversity, which, when human
plans are failing, when health is broken, when
loved ones are in danger, or even when they
are taken from us, can still look up and say :

> God's greatness flows around our incompleteness,
> Round our restlessness, His rest,
> And every cloud that floats above
> And veileth love—itself is love.

Patience, moreover, that reaches to eternal hope
for the race, believing that God is Love, and
that love never faileth ; that love omnipotent
possesses resources and operations whereby frozen
hearts, defective wills, stiffened impenitencies
shall be brought home at last to His heart, and
that

> . . . Somehow good
> Shall be the final goal of ill,
> To pangs of nature, sins of will,
> Defects of doubt and taints of blood.

The supreme importance, then, the wonderful
appropriateness of this injunction, " Add to your
patience godliness," at this particular step in
St. Peter's category, is immediately obvious.
This patience, this resting in the Lord, this
utter emancipation from pessimism, this com-

plete satisfaction with God's wise, pure will, if it is quietistic, indolent, merely an intellectual recreation, is nothing but a lamentable self-deception. The one solid proof of its being is action, and its mode of action is godliness. Godliness is optimism gone to work, it is patience shining out, it is submission conditioning itself in achievement, it is " rest in the Lord " reaching forth into restless activity for man, for godliness is " God-likeness." The only true test of resting in the Lord is that they who thus rest are slowly transformed into the image of Him in whom they rest. Complacent intellectual assent to philosophic theories about the Absolute and the Universal Soul is not godliness. A dream, a theory, a dogma will never save a soul alive. The Father of the spirits of men is not a doting dispenser of irrational caresses, interposing to prevent the natural consequences of selfish, un-progressive, unhelpful, ungodly lives. Any theory of the relation between God and man that does not include godliness, which represents what it calls salvation as a scheme for rescue from well-deserved after-death correction, is simply one more appeal to the calculating self-love of men. God's salvation is no such immoral mockery ; it is a vital force, slowly transforming character, or it is a delusion ; it is an evolving impulse, changing hearts, checking propensities, forming God-likeness, or it is a baseless fabric of a dream. The true test of the growth of the God-like character is, without doubt, its progress along the whole line of human life, the whole range of human experience ; it fertilizes the whole field of a man's being ; where it is growing it slowly makes manhood manlier, womanhood nobler and more adorable, home happier, business cleaner, temper sweeter, desires more regulated. It cannot be hid. It not only unfolds all that is sweetest and best in the individual man or woman, it also shines out and blesses others. Now, as godliness is God-likeness, I am quite certain that it cannot be otherwise than a profitable exercise for all of us that we should test our conception of the character of God, which is the basis of patience, by an inquiry as to the growth of this God-likeness. To gaze mentally into God, says St. Paul, or, as he calls it, " to behold with unveiled face " the glory of the Lord, is to assimilate the Divine likeness, or, as St. Paul expresses it, " to be transformed into the same image."

It is a profound idea this " gazing into God," this mental idealizing of an Infinite and universal creative self-consciousness, and it is best accomplished by mentally analyzing His self-revelation in the Incarnation. St. John, who most intimately knew that self-revelation, who lay on His bosom and shared His thoughts, has analyzed the essence of the Divine nature with regard to its metaphysical, intellectual, and practical character, and has given a definition of each. He

says, God is Spirit, that is the metaphysical;
God is Light, that is the intellectual; God is
Love, that is the practical. And by this analysis
the human standard of God-likeness must be
measured. Godliness is reflecting, in some degree, in ourselves the same characteristics. God-
likeness, as to the first, the metaphysical essence
of God, is automatic. God is Spirit. Man is
spirit. I cannot define spirit; but spirit is the
eternal substance out of which all individual
forms of existence emerge. Man, tracked to the
centre of his being, is also spirit, because man
is the offspring of God. The thought is stupen-
dous, anti-materialistic, influential. But it is
not an attainment, it is an endowment. In
that respect man's God-likeness, or godliness,
is irrevocable and indestructible. " I have said
ye are gods, ye are all the children of the Most
High." It is at once man's dignity, man's
danger, and man's eternal hope. Obviously, to
know it and to live it, as the pattern Son knew
it and lived it, would be to have arrived at the
fulfilment of the prophecy, " Ye shall be perfect
as your Father which is in heaven is perfect."
But that is not yet. Meanwhile the minutest
realization of it, the vaguest conception that
the pure and awful life of God is embedded
in our inmost self, deeply rebukes the lower
nature, the seat of appetite and passion, ennobles
life, and enlarges our capacity for God. It is
well often to repeat solemnly and with inten-

tion : " Know ye not that your bodies are
Temples of the Holy Ghost ?" and " Christ in
you, the hope of glory."

God is Light. That is St. John's conception of
the intellectual essence of God. A beautiful, a
comprehensive analogy, appropriate because light
is a mystery, as God is a mystery. Though the
most familiar, light is at the same time the
least understood of natural phenomena. Indeed,
modern science denies its objective existence,
declaring it to be the activity of millions of
undulating waves, causing vibrations which im-
pinge on a faculty, and produce an impression
called light. The analogy is as old as human
history. The very word " God " is derived
from a Sanskrit word meaning " the shining."
Light in the physical world symbolizes the intellectual action, the thought-action of God in
the spiritual world. Light produces colour, destroys deadly bacilli, unifies chemical opposites,
becomes the source of power when liberated
from coal, blinds the eye to other things. Light
is palpable, refreshing, educative, glorious, life-
giving, and at the same time indefinable. Now,
I ask myself with some apprehension, Where
is my God-likeness ? " Ye are the light of the
world," said Jesus ; " let your light so shine."
Whom are we enlightening ? Into what darkened, sorrow-stricken hearts are we bringing
the light of consolation, sympathy, trust ? Into
what profound midnight of moral rottenness are

we pouring the light of truth, of purity, of rectitude ? What young life are we illuminating
with the light of our own experience, that their
feet may not stumble as ours have stumbled ?
Light is God's remedy for human depravity.
It is the means whereby men see things as they
are, and, as Tennyson says, " We must needs
love the highest when we see it." It is light,
knowledge, truth, reality that regulates brute
instincts and drives away antiquated superstitions. " Where there is no vision of God," in
other words, where there is no light, " the people
perish." Why, then, is it so difficult to stir up
healthy, enthusiastic interest in the Church's
mission work, in her clear commission to be a
light to lighten the Gentiles ? Why is it almost
impossible in a somewhat isolated parish, like
St. John's, Westminster, to obtain the services
of Sunday school teachers, light-bearers for little
unlighted souls ? Why do I appeal again and
again in vain to such a congregation as this for
district visitors ? Allowing a vast discount for
those whose duties honestly do not admit it,
it is because professing Christians, in whose
individual souls the light of the supernatural is
kindled, who are themselves rejoicing in the
light of the knowledge of God, will not be a
witness to men of the God-light that shines in
themselves. They will not, so far as this aspect
of the God they are to resemble is concerned,
" add to their patience God-likeness."

And, finally, God is Love. This is St. John's analysis of the practical essence of the nature of God. This is the epitome of His character, the all inclusive definition of His attitude towards men. This is the golden clue which saves the anxious heart from losing its way in the labyrinth of tangled theology that surrounds the familiar conception of God.

And God is Love that man may become love; and that we may be under no delusion as to the exact nature of His love, as He has conditioned Himself in natural phenomena that we might recognize Him as the Infinite Mind, so has He conditioned His love, tenderness, sympathy, and self-sacrifice in the workings of the human mind, the words of a human voice, and the actions of a human life in the Incarnation. And as we contemplate Jesus, we are looking on the Sacrament of Love. What are the agony and bloody sweat, the cross and passion, the precious death and burial, but God's picture-lesson of the intensity of His love. In the little cell of the prison of La Roquette in Paris, where the Archbishop was imprisoned before his assassination by the mad fiends of the Commune, was a narrow window in the thickness of the door, shaped like a Calvary cross. The Archbishop scratched with a nail over each extremity of the cross one of the well-known words applied by St. Paul to the love of God—breadth, length, depth, height : *latitudo, longitudo, profunditas, sublimitas.*

12

He was drinking of the cup that his Master
drank of, but he knew that the love of God
revealed in the mystery of the cross was immeasurably greater than the passing mystery of
evil ; that it was the pledge of the ultimate
ascension of humanity beyond the reach of pain
and sorrow ; the promise of the Omnipotent
Father that evil should not exist an instant
beyond the time that He has set wherein to
work by it a greater good. The love of Jesus,
then, is the sacrament of the love of God ; therefore godliness is Christ-likeness, likeness to Jesus.
Add to your patience Christ-likeness, not by
copying a model, but by sharing a life. We
could not copy Jesus if we tried, but we can
unfold the Jesus character which is infolded in
our being.

And I believe that the Jesus character, which
is God-likeness, is mainly unfolded in the simple
details of daily life. I am sure it is more
frequently stifled in these details. Daily self-
centredness, daily indulgence of the fleshly
appetites, jealousy, detraction, irritability, mean-
ness—these warp the higher nature more surely
than greater falls. Such a life is not inconsistent with much outward respectability and a
reputation for religion, but it is fatal to godliness.

Godliness, then, is a vital force and not a
religious phrase. It is God's indwelling Spirit
moving in the soul and building character. With
watchful, prayerful culture it will transfigure

life. As Spirit, as Light, as Love, it will lead
you out of selfishness into Divine altruism to
take your part in all remedial work for your
fellow-men, and in aggressive warfare against
the preventable causes of the multitudinous
miseries of mankind. In proportion to the
clearness of your own vision of the character of
God in whose image you are made, and to whose
image you are predestined to be conformed,
will be the measure of your power to counteract
the restless sobbing of humanity of which you
are a part, and without which you cannot yourself enter into full salvation ; for in its extended
meaning God's Christ includes the whole race of
which He Himself is the Soul and the Life.
Let us labour, then, to add to our patience godliness. And not only will the world be better
that we have lived, but we shall have had our
share in promoting that " one far-off Divine
event to which the whole creation moves,"
and that is the ultimate complete salvation of
the whole race, which is the irresistible purpose
of the Father, for " of Him, and through Him,
and to Him are all things, to Whom be glory
for ever and ever. Amen."

BROTHERLY KINDNESS:
The Road to Love.

"Add to your godliness love of the brethren; and to your love of the brethren love."—2 *Peter* i. 7.

SO the topmost rung of the golden ladder of human progress is Love. It is not possible to climb higher. This is the final glory of the soul, the full completion of the purpose of God, what the Buddhist calls Nirvana and the Christian calls Heaven, namely, complete identification with Universal Life, and Universal Life is God, and God is Love. To this perfect consummation the whole of human education, with all its varied experiences and conditions and perplexities, is irresistibly advancing. God is Love, and Love never faileth; and Love cannot give less than all to the object of affection, and Love's all is Himself—God's self. I invite you in times of inevitable depression to "lift up your eyes to the hills whence cometh your strength"; one illuminating beam from the full sunlight of this knowledge that God is Love puts to flight the dark shadows of pessimism, and bases assurance on an impregnable foundation.

Faith, Hope, and Love were questioned what they thought.
Of future glory which religion taught.
Now Faith believed it firmly to be true,
And Hope expected so to find it, too ;
Love answered, smiling with a conscious glow,
" Believe ? expect ? I KNOW it to be so."

It is not, however, this glorious final consummation, to be completed in the future, when
God shall be all and in all, that is our subject
to-day, but the road to it. And in that we are
every one of us deeply interested and concerned.
The process of race development is the same
as the process of individual development. It is
not effected by violent interposition from without ; it is the slow self-evolution of a Divine
germ from within. It is through the gradual
assimilation by the community of Christian
principles, which slowly shape human government, pervading all departments of social life,
influencing public opinion and the conduct of
man to man. And the principle which lies at
the root of race development is " love of the
brethren," or, as the old version translated it,
" brotherly kindness." St. Peter's injunction,
" Add to your godliness brotherly kindness,"
may sound hackneyed and commonplace, but it
is in reality the only leverage power that will
ever lift the race. Consider the emphasis of the
command, " Add to your godliness brotherly
kindness." Godliness, God-likeness, the transformation of the individual into the likeness of
the Divine character, is indeed a noble attain-

ment, but it may be marred by selfishness, by
isolation, aloofness. Naturally its first action is
to fertilize the being of its possessor ; to make
him holier, happier, purer ; but it must be
rescued from the taint of individualism, or it
will warp down the character into that most
unlovely thing, a narrow, isolated religious bigot.
It must be " added to "; it must reach out to
bless and vitalize others. The least light from
God's heart that has advanced your own Godward growth is yours in trust for others ; you
must communicate it ; you must " add to your
godliness brotherly kindness." Now, obviously,
this brotherly kindness is something more influential, more practical, than mere sentiment.
It is not fulfilled by that feeble and fluctuating
philanthropy the product of which is called " a
good-natured man." It must be based on the
central truth revealed by the Christ of the essential brotherhood of the human race ; it implies
obligation to God because He is the Father
of humanity, and obligation to humanity because
it is the son of God.

It is marred, it is denied when you narrow
down brotherhood to the community of the
converted, to the number of the baptized, to
the handful who agree in theological opinion.
To " add to your godliness brotherly kindness "
is to realize the responsibilities attaching to race
brotherhood because you have incorporated
universal Fatherhood into the verities of your

religious belief. Our temptation is to cry : " Such knowledge is too wonderful and excellent for me ; I cannot attain unto it ; the difficulties of applying the truth practically to the international and social perplexities of the world are so great that it becomes only a counsel of perfection, a shadowy ideal." The difficulties are obvious, and the slowness of the remedial action of this truth is wearisome ; but, nevertheless, it is God's way of working, and from the recognition of this truth, sometimes very dim, and from the action of this truth, sometimes very tardy, every reform has arisen in the past, and from it every step of progress will proceed in the future. Nothing can compensate for the absence of the moral power which this truth, and this truth alone, can breathe into every department of national life. The heroic act of self-judgment by which this nation freed itself from the shame and sin of the slave trade was based not on mere philanthropy and compassion, but on the recognition of the essential truth, " a man, and therefore a brother." Godly men, deeply convinced, " added to their godliness brotherly kindness," and by their earnestness and patient perseverance influenced public opinion till the national conscience was awake.

Only thus, by the recognition of the equal dignity, destiny, and sonship of men, will the burden and disgrace of war between civilized races, and the animosities arising from the social

problems of the day, give place to international
concord and confidence between different classes
of the community. We shall not live to see it,
though, like John the Baptist, we may prepare
the way for it ; but some day the God-inspired
cry shall ring through the hearts of men, " Sirs,
ye are brethren," and God shall give to all
nations " unity, peace, and concord."

　And it is just here that the very humblest
can do his part. The great consummation called
Love, when God shall be all in all, can only come
by the slow growth of public opinion ; and public
opinion is the result of individuals severally becoming convinced of the truth of a principle,
and acting upon it in the commonplace events of
human social life. It is possible for you and
for me, resolutely and with clear conviction, to
" add " to such godliness as we may have attained " brotherly kindness " by deliberately
adopting before God the brotherhood standard
in our dealings with, and our judgment of,
our fellow-men. Even Freemasonry, one of the
oldest brotherhoods in the world, though only
a travesty of the brotherhood of the race, has
power to overcome private hatreds and race
animosities. Read in the thirty-third verse of the
twentieth chapter of the first Book of Kings
how Ahab, King of Israel, was compelled to spare
the life of Benhadad, King of Syria, because
the sign of a Master Mason passed between
them. Even the brotherhood of the Anarchist,

the Fenian, and the Communist recognizes its obligations. Carlyle, in his history of the French Revolution, tells us how a well-dressed man slipped off his coat and waistcoat, and rushed to help in erecting a barricade, and when a voice cried out, " Your watch and purse are on the ground," replied, " A man's watch and purse are safe with his brothers "; and they were safe. Such brotherhoods, with all their exaggerations and earthly motives, are a standing reproach to professing Christians. The forgotten Freemasonry of the race is Divine sonship, and the neglected Freemason's sign is the sign of the cross, and the hand-grip of brotherly kindness. The Blessed Sacrament is the Grand Lodge of the Order, for it is the proclamation that the race is redeemed, and that humanity in solidarity is the Body of the Lord. When men stand by their family, they say blood is thicker than water ; but the blood of Christ was shed to demonstrate that the golden link of brotherhood in God's universal family is more binding in His sight than the accident of a common birth ; and though we cannot, as individuals, abolish war and solve the social problems of the age, and bring on the millennium in a hurry, we can remember that the men we meet in the street, and amongst whom our lives are spent, are our brothers, and that cool indifference to the interests of others, and the ready-tongued murder of the reputations of those we hardly know by name, and the miserable tale-bearing and slandering that disfigure Christian communities, is fratricide—sheer fratricide. It is our brother whom we are slaying ; and however broad may be our phylacteries, our " godliness " is the merest trash until, in the spirit of St. Peter's injunction, we have " added to our godliness brotherly kindness."

The incidents of the Holy Week, through which we are passing, contain God's inspired picture-lesson of the working out of " brotherly kindness " in the one perfect Elder Brother of the race. The Eternal Word, that part of God which utters itself, conditions itself in .created things, distinct from God and yet one with Him —just as your conception of yourself is distinct from yourself, and yet is not an independent existence—the Eternal Word " thought it not a thing to be grasped at " (says the Epistle), to abide inert and unmanifested in the universal life of Godhead while a whole race of sons needed a stimulus, but voluntarily individualized Himself in human conditions, " emptied Himself " of infinite attributes, and became the man Jesus ; and in this form, as perfect man, completely atoned, at-oned human will and self-consciousness to the high and perfect will of God, and so offered to the Father, in the name of the race, that perfect holiness, purity, self-forgetfulness, obedience, for which the Fatherhood of the Creator yearns. This deep, beautiful hunger of God for the perfection of His sons is the only element in God's nature that requires propitiating. And the satisfaction of this hunger was the propitiatory sacrifice offered by Christ. But His message to the race of which He is the Elder Brother is : " You also shall, each one of you, similarly propitiate the hungering love of the Father ; the power by which I did it is in measure in each one of you, for I, the Word, am the Germ, the Inmost, the Hope of Glory in each one of you : but you must let the mind that was in Me be in you also "—that is, you must have a mind to do it, wish to do it, will to do it ; stir up the gift that is within thee ; give the Divine nature a chance ; with thine own hand pluck up the weeds that choke its growth ; smite that lower carnal self of thine, that vanity, envy, temper, self-indulgence, pride, indolence ; have a mind to empty thyself of self-fulness. And wouldst thou know thyself ? Well did Juvenal say, " From heaven descended that word, ' Know thyself.' " Wouldst thou know thyself ? Follow to Calvary, tread where He trod ; in imagination, that is, lay down the motives and principles that guide thy life side by side with that yielded will of perfect sonship, and see how much of His mind you share, what likeness there is to that image to which you are predestined to be conformed. There is no other road to brotherly kindness than the will to walk it—" Let this mind be in you."

It is time that some of us woke up, and Holy
Week is the annual call to awakening. May I
not invite you to spend it, not in maudlin
sentimentality over the wrongs of a Sinless
Sufferer, but in earnest consideration of the
attitude of His mind as the God-sent sample of
perfect sonship, and in stern, resolute deter-
mination to " let this mind be in us which was
also in Christ Jesus," and with the prayer :
" That it may please Thee to give us true re-
pentance, to forgive us all our sins, negligences,
and ignorances, and to endue us with the grace
of Thy Holy Spirit to amend our lives according
to Thy Holy Word. We beseech Thee to hear
us, good Lord."

OUR FATHER WHICH ART IN HEAVEN.

" After this manner therefore pray ye : Our Father which art in heaven."—*Matt.* vi. 9.

IT is not my intention to analyze the Paternoster, the guild-prayer of Christendom, that which the early Church called the *Oratio Quotidiana*, textually, historically, or critically. I desire to consider it esoterically and ethically, and to deepen, if possible, my own sense of responsibility as one of the age to whom has been committed the priceless treasure of the most recent self-revelation of God, namely, a reasonable, acceptable, unterrifying concept of the Absolute, and His relation to humanity.

The Paternoster gathers up the Godward thoughts of the ages and focuses them upon one transcendent aspect of the Divine nature. It bids us cease from mentally pursuing an unthinkable abstraction through boundless space, or trembling before an omnipotent autocrat on a sapphire throne beyond the stars, and it bids us speak into the immensity whence we came the trusting, affectionate word, " Father." And inasmuch as it is a recognized axiom that nothing

can come home to the human mind except as it
is described in terms of human experience, this
concept, given to us authoritatively from the
fountain head, though confessedly human and
obviously inexhaustive, is enough for the soul's
peace.

Seventeen years ago, in Boston, I was con-
versing with Dr. Oliver Wendell Holmes, a far-
sighted, well read, reverent-minded disciple of
science. The vast stock of human speculations
upon religious questions was familiar to him.
Though of advanced age, his mind was clear and
analytical, and he told me that the whole of his
religious conviction was now centred, with an
intensity he found it difficult to describe, in the
first sentence of the Paternoster, " Our Father
which art in heaven." " Divest it," he said,
" of the accretions which have gathered round
it, of the limitations which have obscured its
comprehensiveness, and it satisfies wholly such
measure of capacity for apprehending God as is
vouchsafed to man." This witness is true ; for
the God-conception embodied in the Paternoster
supplements, amplifies, fulfils the God-conceptions of all previous generations, and, without
contradicting what was relatively true in each
of them, differentiates the Christian revelation
from all of them ; for the transcendent disclosure
of Universal Fatherhood in the invocation, " Our
Father which art in heaven," embraces the whole
world, declaring that there is neither yellow

man nor black man, neither Greek nor Jew,
circumcision nor uncircumcision, barbarian, Scy-
thian, bond nor free, but that the Christ, the
Divine Humanity, the Pattern Son, is " all and
in all," and therefore that the whole human
family, the sum total of human flesh and blood,
in all ages and of all conditions, is the offspring
of God and possesses an hereditary right to call
God Father.

It has been the fashion to say that the Paternoster was not original ; that it was plagiarized
from an ancient Hebrew formula. The suggestion
may be dismissed. The best scholars deny it.
Dean Alford assures us that there is no evidence
existing to prove it. Bishop Lightfoot declares
that the statement was based upon a few un-
important and commonplace parallels. No ; the
Paternoster came as a surprise. The inferences
implied in it aroused at once the interest of the
thinkers, and the antagonism of the formalists.
It was a surprise, as the flower on the century
plant is a surprise : an evolution and yet a
contrast. An evolution, inasmuch as all previous
God-conceptions were a prelude to this great
unveiling ; a surprise, inasmuch as none of these
conceptions had arrived at predicating the inseverability of God and man implied in the
Paternoster. There is a science called " comparative theology." When it is carried into the
dim ages of the past, and the slow evolution of
the religious instinct in the human race is studied,

without narrowness and prejudice, it is clear that all the upward aspirations of men were preparatory to the great disclosure of the Paternoster. Thoughtful students have traced the inscribed records of these aspirations through the history of three great and independent races, having no common parentage and no common language, and all anterior to Judaism ; the Egyptian, the Semitic Chaldean, and the Aryan Indian—and the independent search of the thinkers of these races after the Supreme Intelligence has left behind it, amidst some profound misconceptions, ideas of imperishable beauty. These records are accessible and generally authentic. The least dependable, perhaps, are the Indian Vedas, which have come down to us in manuscript, written by a reed upon the leaves of plants. In Mesopotamia we can actually handle the original documents in baked clay bricks, precisely in the same condition in which they left the hand of the inscriber. In Egypt we have the original papyri. In India, the religious conceptions based upon the Vedas still remain. Not so with the others ; the culture, the language and religion of Mesopotamia and ancient Egypt are dead. But all the records of these great races are evidences of the heart of man turning to God as the flower turns to the sun. That which they had was a revelation sufficient for the age, and ever and anon some one greater than his contemporaries, in advance of his age,

some thinker, some vision seer, collected and
arranged the perceptions and affirmations of his
time and lifted the moral and spiritual sense of
the community, and made easier the future
evolution of Godward thought.   Who these
pioneers were in the very distant past we know
not ; but we do know of Moses, Zoroaster, Confucius, the Hindoo sages, Buddha, Pythagoras,
Socrates, Plato.   And then ! Then " the fulness of time " was come ; the moment in history
had arrived when the Creative Soul would give
a complete answer to all the upward aspirations
of men.   Forth from the Infinite intensity comes
One whose life was an unveiling of the moral
nature of the Absolute.   He enunciated no system of philosophy ; He advanced no scientific
argument ; He founded no school of theology ;
He simply proclaimed from His direct knowledge,
from His inmost consciousness, " I am the Son
of the Father God."   I know it, because in Me
the Divine and the human are at-oned.   But I am
a manifestation in time relations of a universal
truth.   Ye also are sons as I am.   Sonship
is a fact of your being, though not yet a fact
of your consciousness.   What you are is a fact
of your being.   What you know of what you
are will be the gradual instructing of your consciousness.   Man and his consciousness are not
necessarily co-extensive.   The road to this knowledge is doing the will ; do the will and you shall
know the doctrine.   Meanwhile you are sons as

13

I am; " I in God, you in Me," humanity potentially " perfect in One." Therefore when ye
pray, say " Our Father which art in heaven."

Pause for a moment mentally to estimate Him
who thus spake. The occasion of the giving of
the Paternoster was that His disciples had seen
Him praying, and had asked Him to teach them
thus to pray. He gives them the form ; He cannot yet unveil the immeasurable inwardness of
the words. Now, to the believer in the revelation
that Jesus represented " all the fulness of the
Godhead bodily " the endeavour to realize how
He could pray, and to whom He could pray,
imposes almost a breaking strain upon the
thinking capacity. But we must try and think
into it. He told us to think Him ! He asked
what men did think of Him. And thought, blundering into expression through the poor expedient
of language, replies : Jesus was God in the sense
of His being the highest manifestation of the
Absolute capable of being apprehended by finite
minds. That He was not the exclusive or the
exhaustive manifestation of the Absolute He
Himself warned us when He said, " The Father
is greater than I "; in other words, the Absolute
is greater than even its highest manifestation ;
and as your thought of yourself is one with yourself, and yet is apart from yourself, so this
supremest thought of the Absolute called Jesus
was one with the Absolute, and yet apart from
the Absolute. In the language of philosophy,
God's thought of Himself is the Logos, the Word

in self-utterance ; when He thinks that thought it becomes differentiated into the visible universe and man. The supremest thought of God is the Archetypal Perfect Man, Jesus. So Jesus is the objective manifestation of that subjective Logos which is immanent in all men ; therefore, as this oneness of God with humanity was intuitively apprehended by the consciousness of Jesus, His praying would have been a forceful blending of His innermost being with the universal mind (He Himself called it " the Father within Me "), a mental absorption into the Absolute so intense that it would have visibly affected His physical frame and attracted the attention of bystanders. We read on another occasion that " as He was praying the fashion of His countenance was altered," and this surely prompted the request, " Lord, teach us to pray." And the reply would have been, though not these words, virtually in this sense : Not yet can I teach you thus to pray ; " as the Father knoweth Me, even so know I the Father "; it is not so, as yet, with you. You, as infants in the new school, know not yet what ye are ; the time shall come when ye shall worship the Father in spirit and in truth, as I worship Him. Meanwhile, the road to this knowledge is through trust, love, forgiveness, kindness, helpfulness, even to enemies ; therefore, though as yet ye cannot know all that it means, when ye pray, say " Our Father which art in heaven."

13—2

Now the main proposition which I desire to emphasize, as a corrective to that indifference that arises from familiarity, is the incomparable importance of the Paternoster as marking an epoch in the self-revelation of the Infinite Mind. and the corresponding weight of the responsibility that rests upon the recipients of the revelation. It is not possible to overstate the influence upon humanity of its conception of its God. Our Lord emphasized the distinction between the ethical consequences of the Deistic concept and the Paternal concept in His words : " Whosoever killeth you shall think that he doeth God service, and this shall they do because they know not the Father." God believed in, Fatherhood unknown, has been the origin of some of the blackest crimes against humanity that have ever disgraced the world. Deism, or God believed in as the Autocrat of the Heavens, and Fatherhood unknown, is a far more cruel religious conception than Pantheism. Pantheism, though in the Indian philosophy it identified God with the universe, was a fascinating, elevating conception. It could never have produced the horrors of the Spanish Inquisition. It was a calming, unifying thought that the Universal Soul was the most uplifting energy in everything ; but it was a vague generality, without character or differentiation, and Deism was its reaction ; and Deism banishes God from all real contact with humanity, except as inexorable lawgiver and judge ; and the very despotism and autocracy of the conception of Deism made even good men despotic and autocratic and hard-hearted. The revelation of the Paternoster corrected the vagueness of Pantheism, and obliterated the aloofness of Deism, and assured us that the Universal Soul stood to us in a relationship which is at the root of our idea of Fatherhood ; that He was lovingly responsible for human existence and education, and that though the true extent of the relationship which is brought home to us by the use of the word " Father " cannot be realized by our present consciousness, we are justified in a tranquil self-abandonment to His responsibility, His power, and His love.

Two thousand years have passed since Deism was dethroned by the Paternoster. Has this new concept convinced the world that humanity is a corporate unity, an organic whole, thought into being by the self-evolving Father Spirit, of which corporate unity each individual item is under the sacred obligation of brotherhood to the rest ? Is the lesson learnt ? It has been perfectly learnt and nobly practised by a few isolated thinkers and doers down the pages of history : reformers, emancipators, inspirers of social duty. Every step in the amelioration of the condition of humanity is the result of the abolition of Deism and the enthronement of Fatherhood. But to the collective conscience

of the world and of the Church the ethics of
the Paternoster have fallen still-born. Nation
rises against nation ; the press of the world
rings with wars and rumours of wars ; the prevailing theologies still see on the throne of the
universe an omnipotent despot who will doom
the vast majority of His wretched subjects to
everlasting fire ; social evils that undermine the
moral progress of the masses are pampered and
upheld by a Christian legislature if they represent sufficient political power ; environments
still exist in great cities which are a shame and
a curse to our vaunted civilization. And while
we tremble at the indifference of Christian nations
to the obvious obligations of the Paternoster,
and remember our Lord's startling utterance,
" If I had not come and spoken unto them they
had not had sin, but now they have no cloke
for their sin," we are filled with wonder that an
inspired dictum from the World's Creator should
be capable of such signal failure.

Now, there are two considerations which tend
to rebuke this temptation to pessimism. The
first is the total inability of our finite minds to
estimate what in reality is a " long time." Is
two thousand years a " long time "? Succession
of events that appear very slow to our consciousness are not slow upon the plane of the
real. It is only in accordance with our human
standard of measurement that it is a " long
time " since the Paternoster was proclaimed.

How many ages passed while the God-conception of the race evolved through Fetichism, Animism, Totemism, Pantheism, Polytheism, Monotheism, to Deism ? Shall we say ten million years ? Probably far more. Time duration is one of the educative illusions of human life ; it is an arbitrary standard anyhow ; it is a purely empirical, though universally entertained, concept of the human mind. The Universal Father Mind, as the Book of Wisdom says, " reaches from one end to another, mightily and smoothly and sweetly ordering all things," and is not under the limitations of what we call time.

But there is another consideration, and it is this. Possibly you believe in a coming millennium on earth. I do not. I cannot but remember that the temptation which was resisted by the Incarnate One in the wilderness was precisely that for which His loving human heart must have yearned, namely, to establish a kingdom of heaven upon this planet. If with His perfect control of natural law, and abnormal psychic power, He had descended into Jerusalem as a manifest Theophanie, humanity would have been stirred and startled into submission, and all hearts and intellects would have been subdued to Him, and the unrest and disorder and crime and violence and physical suffering of the world would have been under His control, and earth would have been transformed into a Paradise.

The temptation must have been real and intense beyond the power of expression. But the mission of the Christ was not this. " My kingdom is not of this world," He said. His kingdom is in the fuller, freer, completer world, for enjoyment of which, life in this world is but the education, the school. The potentiality for the inheritance of this kingdom is within the individual : " The kingdom of heaven is within you "; and the profound, the esoteric application of the Paternoster is not primarily to the external conditions of earthly life as a whole, but to the heart of each individual human being. While the awakening of the Divine consciousness in individual human beings necessarily leavens, brightens, purifies the world in which they live, and makes others happier, the true kingdom of heaven is within. The key to the inner secret of the Paternoster is that every individual is a microcosm, a little world ; and each clause of the prayer applies to the inmost secret in each one. And the more profoundly you think it out, the more luminous will the fact become to you that the secret of humanity is the deeply-buried interior kingdom of heaven in each separate individual, and that he who opens his soul inwardly, through his reason and affection, to the stirring of the life of God within, is doing all that his Father God requires of him in this world, for he is arriving at the outer fringe of the secret of Jesus when He said, " The Father

in Me doeth the works," and he is approaching,
only as yet approaching, the inner meaning of
the injunction of the Paternoster :

" WHEN YE PRAY, SAY OUR FATHER WHICH ART
IN HEAVEN."

HALLOWED BE THY NAME.

" Hallowed be Thy Name."—*Matt.* vi. 9.

NAMES are in all cases significant : they are symbols and expressions. There is a considerable literature on the subject of names ; their observation, study, and analysis often lead to discoveries in history and in folk-lore of the greatest interest. For example : the name of Washington, the capital of the United States, is derived from George Washington, the first President, and his name was derived from a village in the county of Durham, where his ancestors lived ; and this village obtained its name from the Wasings, an ancient Teutonic clan. Names, when not significant of locality, are all significant of character, and in ancient days were constantly compounded of some name of the Deity. The names of the Assyrian kings were all compounded of the name of the Assyrian god ; and most of the Hebrew names contain the higher Hebrew name of God, El ; thus Joel means the Lord is God ; Elijah, compounded of El and Jahveh, means God is the Lord. The recognized significance attaching to names immeasurably enhances the importance of the first petition in the Paternoster : " Hallowed be Thy Name." He who was the Perfect Sacrament of the Absolute, and the Ideal Representative of our race, at a given moment in history presented to the God-consciousness of humanity a reasonable concept of the Creative Soul, calculated to correct the vagueness of Pantheism on the one hand, and obliterate the aloofness of Deism on the other. And this He did by bidding us speak into the unthinkable vital intensity a name, a homely name, a significant name—the name Father : " When ye pray, say Our Father . . . hallowed be Thy Name."

No study in the history of human psychology is more profoundly interesting, nothing more clearly indicates the successive stages of human God-conception in response to Divine self-revelation, than the various names applied to the Eternal Being. A thing is to a man's mind what he names it ; the name of God in each age and nation was an indication of the human concept of the character of God in that age and nation.

You will remember the conundrum proposed in the 30th chapter of the Book of Proverbs : " What is His Name ; canst thou tell ?" That question was a stimulus to thought, a significant appeal to that dim mysterious memory of a higher knowledge once possessed, now lost. Humanity knew the name once, in a bygone existence, before plunging into the sphere of sense, and the conditions of time. Plato was right ; Wordsworth was right :

> The soul that riseth in us, our life's star,
> Hath elsewhere had its setting, and cometh from afar.

Jesus " came out from the Father and came into the world "; and as Jesus and humanity are the same genus, and we were " in Him before the foundation of the world," and as therefore we have the same origin, the same nature, and the same future, we too have " come out from the Father and come into the world "; we too are personal spirits who have proceeded from God into matter (St. Paul says not by our own will), and our past is organically and auto-matically forgotten, leaving only dim and blurred memories, one of which is the ceaseless instinctive mental effort down the ages to discover, or perhaps I ought to say to remember, the name of the Supreme.

> Oft times strange sense have I of this,
> Vague memories that hold me with a spell,
> Touches of unseen lips upon my brow
> Breathing some incommunicable bliss.

The earliest effort of this, called by Plato Anamnesis ; the earliest guess at the recovery of the name that we can trace, long before the Hebrew theocracy, was profoundly reverent in that it was rather a phrase than a name. Parts of the Todtenbuch, or Sacred Book of the Dead, recovered from the Egyptian papyri that are wrapped round the mummy cases, certainly date from the prehistoric stage of Egyptian civilization before the dynasty of Menes, which would place these records at a period six thousand years before the Christian era. The history of Manetho, written by the order of Ptolemy Philadelphus, which dates the dynasty of Menes, was burnt with the Alexandrian library, but sufficient quotations are in existence from it in the writings of Josephus and Eusebius to enable the date of the dynasty of Menes to be decided.

Now, in the Todtenbuch there is no name for God, only a paraphrase. There are several of these paraphrases : " the self-existing one," " the self-becoming one," " the one of ones," " the one without a second," " the becoming from the first," " the one who making all was not made." The oldest definite name, as distinguished from phrase, descriptive of God, is El. Inscriptions found at Larsa, near Ur of the Chaldees, show that four thousand years before Christ, a Semitic population existed at Larsa whose supreme deity was Ila or El, from whose name that of Elohim and Allah was derived by the Hebrews and Arabs respectively. From Larsa the name would have spread to Ur of the Chaldees, where Abraham was born, and from Ur of the Chaldees Abraham would have carried it to the as yet unborn Hebrew race. The various derivatives of this name El, with their special distinctions and significances, Elohim, Elyon, Elshaddai, Eli, and so on, are admirably expounded in Mr. Andrew Jukes' well-known work upon the names of God. Ewald, in his "Lehre von Gott," traces the evolution of the names of God through Israelitish history, distinguishing five names corresponding to five great periods in that history : "the Almighty," the period of the Patriarchs ; "Jehovah," the period of the Covenant ; "God of Hosts," the period of the Monarchy ; "the Holy One of Israel," the period of the later Prophets ; "our Lord" (Adonai), the period of the latest Judaism. And then, to give interpretation, consistency, actuality to every affirmation, every conception, every name hitherto attributed to the Supreme Intelligence, there came forth from the Absolute One, the Revealer of God to man, the Interpreter of man to himself, and He enunciates authoritatively the one and only dogma of Christianity, and embodies it in a Name : "Call no man on earth your father, One is your Father which is in heaven," and "When ye pray, say Our Father . . . . hallowed be Thy Name."

I invite you to consider with me what is implied by hallowing this Name. It is inconceivable that the Incarnate One, who was God come as a Teacher, could have intended to bind our mental conception under a limitation which would have appeared inadequate to the ancient Egyptians six thousand years before Christ.

The new Name must have been intended to
convey a conception of God which would be at
once conservative of His universal immanence
and affirmative of the close intimacy of His
personal contact with the soul of individual man.
To hallow the Name, then, would be, in the first
instance, mentally to guard it against a limiting
anthropomorphism ; to realize that it is not
merely the symbol of a commonplace relationship
implying nothing beyond its literal meaning.
Words, as we know, enlarge their interpretation
in proportion as they are carried to higher planes
of consciousness. It is well to remember that
they have also a tendency to lessen their interpretation, and lose their spiritual force, if they
are habitually used on a lower plane of consciousness. It has happened to many words, in
many languages, in many lands. Names for the
Ruler of the Universe, originating on the higher
plane, intended as a recognition of the sole
sovereignty of the Supreme, have become degraded to lower uses and interpretations. The
Greek word κυριός, the Latin word *Dominus*, the
English word Lord, the German word Herr,
have lost their unique Deistic interpretation ;
and the sovereigns of the last two centuries
have adopted the title of Majesty formerly
reserved for the Deity alone.

Therefore, to " hallow the Name " will be,
in the first instance, while retaining all the
signification of tenderness and responsibility

attaching to the name Father, remembering the
Scripture injunction that the fathers should lay
up for the children, and not the children for the
fathers, to read into it all the higher Godward
thoughts of the past ages of human history,
and especially the profoundly reverent "no
name" of the ancient Egyptians, which was
paraphrazed by special revelation to Moses
when the immanent Life of the Universe was
momentarily revealed to him glowing in the bush.

> Tell them I am, Jehovah said
> To Moses ; while earth heard in dread,
> And smitten to the heart, at once above, beneath, around,
> All nature, without voice or sound, replied, Thou art !

We cannot afford to lose that fascinating
conception of the immanence of the Infinite
Intensity as the only Substance, the Soul, the
" I am " in all that is. To know that Divine
Love, Divine Thought in activity, is the inmost
uplifting energy in everything, simplifies and
facilitates the highest idea of prayer, which is
human thought, full of will, confidence, and
reverence, lifted up, either with or without words,
in harmony with God's ceaseless operations of
benevolent activity. We cannot afford to lose
it ; but we can, so to speak, mentally equip it
to meet the infinite pathos of life by adding
to this Inwardness, this Soul of the Universe,
the revelation of the Paternoster ; hallowing it
by uniting it in thought to the tender, helpful
Name suggestive of responsibility, protection,

relationship. By itself, the " I am " conception
of the Egyptians and of Moses is vague,
perplexing, almost alarming. Interpreted by
the Paternoster, it becomes, if not personal,
certainly individual, and justifies a tranquil self-
abandonment to His power, His responsibility,
His Fatherhood.

Again, to hallow the Name will be to read
into it the transcendent revelation of the character of God enshrined in the definition, " God
is Love." Love is the highest name of God,
but Love is an abstract principle. If the invocation of the Paternoster had been addressed to
an abstract principle, the conception of relationship would have been imperilled. So our Lord,
that the idea of relationship may be clear, precise, and conceivable, embodies it by metaphor
into the concrete. Human fatherhood, alas, is
not always synonymous with love. It is well to
know that the revealed personal name of the
Absolute, namely, Father, is hallowed by that
all-inclusive definition of His character, " God
is Love."

Once more. To hallow the Name is to make
it known. How ? How did the Revealer of the
Name make it known ? He said, " I have made
known Thy Name." How did He make it
known ? Not by argument, oratory, or dogma.
He lived it. Out of His interior knowledge He
first claimed it, repudiating earthly parentage as
a mere metaphor. He then rested the evidence

14

of the truth of what He claimed, upon the testimony of the life He lived. " Show us the
Father," they said. Virtually His answer was :
Live as if God were your Father and you will
know the Father ; live as such a Father's son
ought to live—lovingly, fraternally, forgivingly,
helpfully, kindly to all, enemies included, and
you will have " shown the Father "; others will
believe that God is your Father, and you will
have hallowed His Name.

Lastly, to " hallow the Name " is to keep in
mind—(I do not say that we can do more than
keep in mind, for such knowledge is too wonderful and excellent for us, we cannot attain unto it)
—to keep in mind the profound inwardness of the
Paternoster as finding its complete fulfilment
within each individual human being. Our Lord's
words, " the Father in Me," is the key to this
inwardness that we should keep in mind.
" As He is, so are we in this world "; potentially
as He is, not as yet actually. In the previous
sermon I spoke of Him praying to the Father.
When His perfect at-one-ment between the
human and the Divine was in full realization,
Jesus praying to the Father would have been a
profound interior blending of Spirit with Spirit.
When, under the stress of great physical pain
and mental anguish, the claims of the human
nature, not fully glorified till after physical
death, were paramount, His praying would have
been an illustration of a mental transaction

between different spheres of consciousness. That part of Him which He called " My life," My psychical part (the Greek word is *psuche*), that part of Him which was " exceeding sorrowful even unto death," that division of man which is, as the philosophers say, on the plane of " idea-tion," the intellectual plane, was appealing intensely to that higher plane, the Divine plane, the plane of pure Spirit, the plane He called " the Father in Me." Once, momentarily, He appears, under the pressure of overwhelming physical agony, to have reverted to the Deistic plane of the Hebrew conception in which He was brought up. It is the only recorded occa-sion on which He addressed the Supreme as God ; and then He did not say El, God, but Eli, My God—" Eli, Eli, lama Sabacthani "; but imme-diately He returned to the spiritual plane in the words, " Father, into Thy hands."

Now, I do not say we can realize this inward-ness. I say we should keep it in mind ; it is always well to have beacon-light ideals. It is interesting to know that this inwardness of the Paternoster is no modern speculation. As early as the year 347 A.D., Cyril of Jerusalem suggests it in his exposition on the occasion of the con-secration of the church erected on the site of the Holy Sepulchre. The year 347 was not far from the fountain head ; the interval of time between the delivery of the Paternoster by our Lord, and the exposition of St. Cyril of Jerusalem,

14—2

was not so great as the interval between the
first setting forth of our English prayer-book
and the present time. St. Cyril directs each
petition of the Paternoster inwards. " Ye," he
says, " are the heaven in which God is." " Pray
that the Father's name may be hallowed in you ;
that His kingdom may come in you "; and so on
to the end of the Paternoster. The inferences
from this exposition are obvious. First, an uplifting of the standard of life. This Love that
loved us into being for an inextinguishable purpose is no feeble sentiment, but a consuming fire.
To violate conscience, to live wilfully below the
implanted standard of right and wrong, is to
unhallow the Name and disgrace the inheritance
to which we are born. Secondly, test every God-
conception of theology by the standard of the
Paternoster. Reject the cold intellectualism
which de-humanizes God till He is only omnipotent will behind natural law, or which over-
humanizes Him, or rather demonizes Him, as
the pitiless despot of the universe, a being to
shudder at and not to love. Believe that though
He is an unthinkable universally diffused individuality, He is your Father ; that His will is
your sanctification ; that the duty of life is
intelligent co-operation with that process of
sanctification ; and that such co-operation will
be a daily hallowing of His Name.

GOD'S KINGDOM.

——

"Thy Kingdom come."—*Matt.* vi. 9.

THIS all-embracing petition in the Paternoster, at once a prayer, a proclamation,
and a prophecy, contains, to those whose vision
is opened, first, the authoritative credential of
optimism, and, secondly, a powerful appeal on
behalf of the Bishop of London's fund.

First, optimism. Unless we were optimists,
London and its problems would madden us. His
is the Kingdom, and the power, and the glory,
for ever and ever. Rooted into the verities of
a man's being, this revelation sweeps away the
despondencies of the human soul. It inspires
man with an unfaltering assurance amidst the
struggles, failures, and disappointments of this
passing, perishing existence. It sums up all
worlds, all beings, all phenomena, under the
central controlling over-rule of the one self-
existing Almighty Fatherhood—" in all, through
all, and above all." I do not mean that the
eager exercise of human thought into the problems surrounding our lives is silenced by this
revelation, but I do mean that all uncertainty

as to ultimate issue is swept away by the
knowledge that His *is* the Kingdom ; that the
whole mystery of evil and all its complicated
cross-working purposes are, in the final resort,
under His absolute and irresistible sway. And
the words, " Thy Kingdom come," are the confident aspiration, in co-operation with which,
every awakened heart will ceaselessly energize,
that the Spirit immanent in all things will subdue
every discord and hasten the " one far-off Divine
event to which the whole creation moves,"
namely, the reconciliation of all things to Himself.

Was this perfect optimism, underlying the
language of the Paternoster, a new teaching two
thousand years ago ? In a sense it was. In a
sense the great unveiling of the Paternoster was,
as I have said, a surprise, as the flower on the
century plant is a surprise ; an evolution and yet
a contrast : an evolution, inasmuch as all previous God-conceptions were preparatory to this
disclosure ; a surprise, inasmuch as none of these
conceptions had arrived at predicating the inseverability of God and man implied in the
Paternoster. The fascinating study of ancient
religions and comparative theology witnesses to
this previous preparation of the thoughts of men
for the reception of the wider truth. In this connection it is important to remember that the
Christian revelation embodied in the Paternoster
can take no place in that which is called the
science of comparative theology. Why not ?

Because the Christian revelation is not a new
religion, but the concentration, the explanation,
and the fulfilment of all religions since the world
was ; indeed, the Christian revelation is not a
religion, but a Person. The Christian revelation
is the specific embodiment, in one human personality, of that principle, that spirit, that Godward instinct that was the inmost uplifting
motive of all the religious conceptions of our
remote predecessors, who, in profoundly differing
environments, were seeking after God " if haply
they might find Him." That Divine Logos, or
self-utterance of the Eternal Reason, which was
Incarnate in Jesus, had always been immanent in humanity, inspiring Godward thought,
assimilating all that was best and noblest
and truest in each age, and carrying it higher,
preparing for the fulness of time. Does anyone
doubt this ? Who then, I ask, inspired Moses
to prefer the life of toil to the luxury of Pharaoh's
court ? The Apostle is bold enough to say " the
Christ "—one thousand years before Jesus was
born. What indwelling spirit of love was grieved
by the hardness of heart of the Israelites in
the wilderness ? Again the Apostle plainly says
" the Christ." Who shall dare to limit the
immanence of the Logos to one race or one age ?
Who, I ask, inspired Buddha to seek to trample
down the human weakness of the flesh ? Who
taught Confucius to elaborate a system of respect
for ancestors and social duties which has lasted

three thousand years ? Who stirred the com-
poser of the Bhagavad Gita to strive to take
the Kingdom of Heaven by force ? What was
the power that enabled Socrates nobly to live
and nobly die ? And, deeper still into the past,
what spirit inspired the ancient sages to elaborate
the Egyptian, Babylonian, Assyrian, and Brah-
manical systems of thought, the purer and
better parts of which will live on for ever ?
Augustine answered the question when he wrote :
" The thing itself which is now called the Christian religion was really known to the ancients,
nor was wanting at any time from the beginning
of the human race until the time that Christ
came in the flesh, from whence the true religion
which had previously existed began to be called
Christian." And Justin Martyr, in his first
Apology, emphasizes the same thought in his
words : " Those who lived according to the
Logos " (that is, of course, those who obeyed the
prompting of this inner guidance) " were really
Christians, as were Socrates and Heraclitus,
and such as resembled them." This Logos, this
spirit immanent in all things, this inmost uplifting motive in the Godward thoughts of men,
was, in the fulness of time, embodied, Incarnate,
in one human personality, who came not to
destroy, but to fulfil, all previous Godward conceptions ; and this, this Person, this Incarnation,
is the Christian revelation of God. And He
taught us authoritatively, dogmatically, that the

nature of God is Spirit, the name of God is Love, and the relation of God to humanity is Paternal; and He bids us lift up our hearts and voices in the words, "Our Father, hallowed be Thy name. Thy Kingdom come."

Let us endeavour to analyze, to outline, this expression, "Thy Kingdom." In my own mind, remembering the principle of evolution, I trace a distinction between the expressions, "Kingdom of God" and "Kingdom of Christ." The unique Incarnation of that spirit of sonship always immanent in the race, whom we call Jesus, enriched human thought with an extended re-velation of the truth about the Kingdom of God. He taught us to recognize the Kingdom of God in what is called creation, or the source of life, in other words, whence we came. He taught us that the secret of the universe in which we are is that it is a sphere of the Kingdom of God. He taught us that the highest plane of the King-dom of God is the interior principle within man. How did He teach us this? He assured us that God is Spirit; not a spirit, not an extraneous isolated spiritual being, but the one only "ousia" or substance, the absolute principle out of which all individual forms of existence emerge; that which we call matter is the pro-jection of the creative thought of this absolute principle into the plane of action. Jesus states the fact. He leaves us to infer the method. The geologists have inferred the method so far as this planet is concerned. It is all perfectly logical, all in sequential order of thought. In the unthinkable past a glowing mass swung off from the central solar system, slowly cooling down. In the protoplasmic slime of this cooling sphere was implanted, involved, the potentiality of what we call life. Through millions of ages, under the Divine law of natural selection, and the survival of the fittest, and the transmutation of species, this Kingdom of God on the lower plane was slowly evolved. Gradually the higher expression of the creative thought of the Absolute appears through anthropoid ape, through prognathous ancestor, until the vehicle is prepared in which the Divine Logos can be so enshrined as to fulfil the predestined purpose of evolution and produce a being who shall be able to respond with complete devotion and recognition to the love of the Parent Source ; and, by an orderly sequence of descent, from all-creating spirit to matter, man is on the earth, and the Kingdom of God is enlarged from the plane of sensation to the plane of intellect. The same Kingdom, the same laws, the same phraseology, but now on a higher plane of interpretation. Man, whose name is derived from *mens*, the mind, which in turn is derived from the Sanskrit *manu*, the thinker, is still under the law of the survival of the fittest ; but the law is liberated from the material plane ; it is now the law of the survival of the fittest in intellect, not the fittest in strength.

The kingdom is now the kingdom of mind, not the kingdom of force. The spade of the excavator, the trained genius of the scientific explorer, the careful student of old MSS. have traced from this point the slow evolution of the religious instincts and the Godward conceptions of the past ages, as the promptings of the indwelling Divine nature gradually awakened in man religious belief as a principle and a standard of conduct. His was the Kingdom during the whole prolonged process, and His Kingdom was coming down the lingering ages, always coming, coming through the law of the survival of the fittest ; that is, the fittest for the intelligence of the worshippers in different ages, until the fulness of time should arrive when the Kingdom should be revealed on the highest plane of all. And then, two thousand years ago, when the ceaseless upward instinct of the race was ripe, He came forth who was the embodiment in a single personality of that Divine sonship which had been striving for expression in all men down the ages. " In these last days " (we read) " God hath spoken unto us by His Son, by Whom He made the worlds "; the same Word, or Logos, who had always been the executive Sovereign of the Kingdom. And He revealed the age-long hidden secret of man. " The Kingdom of God," He said, " is within you." Man is climax of creation. " All the laws of the Kingdom that you have learned on the other planes of consciousness are applicable to the complex mystery of yourself. You, each one individually, you are the Kingdom of Christ. The mystery has been hid from the foundation of the world ; it is now revealed. That which is embodied in Me for your observation is immanent in you. It is the spirit of evolution which will irresistibly, but with infinite patience, effect the moral perfection of those who from all eternity the Father has purposed shall ultimately be sanctified."

Am I not, then, justified in saying that this all-embracing petition in the Lord's Prayer is the authoritative credential of optimism, the revealed silver lining to every cloud ? " Why art thou so full of heaviness, O my soul ; why art thou so disquieted within me ? " All that is, is God's Kingdom. He is enthroned in all; from inmost to outmost one purpose runs, one love pulses. There are no blind forces, no causeless incidents ; all things, even moral evil, disappointment, failure, broken health, physical suffering, all are working for ultimate good under the unerring law of Infinite Love ; and beyond the horizon which our human eyesight cannot pass, beyond the feverish dream of the painful puzzle of this mortal life, the All-Father waits to wipe away tears from all eyes. He whose mind is fixed in the truth of these eternal principles " will not be afraid of any evil tidings, for his heart standeth fast in the Lord," and there will be a whole world of meaning in the words when he prays, " Thy Kingdom come."

It is not difficult to see how, as this interior interpretation of the Kingdom of Heaven, as the immortality of God embodied in man's nature begins to shine into the soul, it suggests the attitude in which life's trials should be faced. Life is not the horrible mockery it would be if we were the products of chance, and were going we knew not whither. When fighting temptation, when enduring hardship, when baffled by circumstances, we can rally back upon the Christian revelation of the Paternoster. " The Kingdom of Heaven is within you." The Divine secret of imperishable life which must ultimately conquer the empire of evil is within us, and the purpose of the Father around us ; for the perfect Elder Brother of the race, Who made the revelation, has left us the never-dying consolation of His words : " Be of good cheer, I have overcome," and you shall overcome ; " Because I live, ye shall live also "; " I go to My Father and your Father "; " I go to prepare a place for you."

But once more. This interpretation is preeminently practical ; for it is obvious that the sole test of a believer's mental grip of this truth will be his willingness to hasten the completion of the Kingdom by his usefulness to humanity.

The only profession of a conviction is its practice. Where there is practice there is no need

of profession. Imagine the mockery of praying
those words, " Thy Kingdom come," and
standing aloof from every enterprize of amelioration in a city like London ! The words, " Thy
Kingdom come," detect and expose insincere,
speculative, theoretical Christianity, as litmus
paper detects acid. Imagine, for example, one
in whom the sentiment and instinct of religion
have been awakened, who is intellectually
attracted by esoteric and philosophic thought,
coming to consult, let us say, that eminent
exponent of practical Christianity, the Apostle
St. James. You can almost hear him ask :
" When you repeat the Paternoster, is it sound
or action, is it creed or conduct, is it word or
power, is it the poor shallow fetish worship of
chattering controversy, or is it unwearied labour
for the social recovery of your brethren in
humanity ? When you look around you at the
suffering mass of human wretchedness and sin,
when you clearly see the obstacles that oppose
its diminution, when you know that the Father's
method of establishing His Kingdom is through
the self-sacrificing efforts of consecrated men
and women who believe in the Kingdom, say
who is better because you repeat the Paternoster
daily ? What are you practically doing in this
monstrous human ant-heap called London to
wipe tears from faces, to remove stumbling-
blocks from lives, to lengthen the Church's arm ?
What ! nothing beyond the grudged shilling in

the collection plate ?   Then " (continues St.
James) " do not dignify your sentiment with
the name of a religion, for ' pure religion and
undefiled before God and the Father is to visit
the fatherless and widows in their affliction.' "

I have a purpose in saying this. It is just
here that the petition in the Paternoster becomes
a powerful plea for the Bishop of London's fund.
The Church is, or ought to be, the leaven of the
State, the salt of society. The State is a vast
organism, and the duty of the Church is to
purify that organism and to counteract any
tendency to exaggerated individualism in its
constituent elements. Every Churchman, as
such, is practically under pledge to live mer-
cifully, fraternally, helpfully. If there is a community on God's earth at this moment which is
bound to aid the weak, it is the Church of England, with her unrivalled position of privilege,
power, and influence, enabling her to take her
place by the side of the working classes in all
times of oppression, sweating, tyranny, and
wrong. If the Church is satisfied with the per-
functory discharge of external duties, if her
energies are wasted in miserable disputes about
ritual, or in picking theological motes out of the
eyes of Dissenters, or in furiously fighting for
her own temporal privileges, instead of boldly
leading every enterprize of amelioration and
salting the national life, she is abnegating the
very function of a national Church, which is the

manifestation of Divine sonship and the affirmation of the equal rights of man. The test of
Churchmanship is something more than accuracy
in credal orthodoxy; it is, first and foremost,
love of the brethren.

I would like to ask every Church member
listening to me now whether he or she has been
to the " sweated industries " exhibition in the
Queen's Hall, Langham Place ? Go there, purchase the book descriptive of the exhibition; or,
still better, let one of the intelligent superin-
tendents show you round, and point out to you
articles of clothing and other things which find
their way into West End shops, and are sold to
the well-to-do, which positively represent the
life blood of the cruelly sweated toilers of the
East End, and have been paid for with pence
when they are sold for pounds. Go there, strive
to realize what it means, and you will come forth
with sorrow in your heart and tears in your
eyes, and a new realization of the bitter wrongs
and disabilities of many of the wage-earning
classes, especially of the women, who are not
protected by trade unions.

I do not pretend that there is any facile or
immediate remedy for this condition of things;
but I am certain that if the Church in her corporate capacity, caring nothing for unpopularity,
presenting a united front, brought her true
weight to bear upon this question of sweating,
and, through her representatives in the House

of Lords, approached the State of which she is an integral part, and promoted in the Upper House, after free consultation with the experts amongst the Labour leaders, some enactment making this horrible sweating impossible, her influence in the councils of the nation would avail to save these suffering brethren of ours from much hardship and injustice. Meanwhile, if every one listening to me now would urgently demand from every West End tradesman some guarantee that the article they purchase has not been produced by sweated labour, the mere inquiry would do good.

Go, I pray you, to this exhibition, and even if you can do nothing to remove the cause of the evil, you will be thrilled with the desire to qualify under the text of St. James, and " visit the fatherless and widows in their affliction."

We all know, and the King of the Kingdom of Heaven knows, that vast numbers who do love the brethren, and to whom the Paternoster is a reality, cannot personally visit the fatherless and widows in their affliction. Their line of duty is obviously elsewhere. The claims of life require them in other directions, but the responsibility remains. What they cannot do themselves they must empower others to do in their names.

The army of the Kingdom of God is not a volunteer army, but under rigid conscription, with the privilege of purchasing a substitute to go down to the battle. To do neither is to court a deserter's fate. 15

An authoritative substitute for personal service makes its claim upon you to-day. It is the organization known as the Bishop of London's fund. The work that it has done, and is doing, in this vast city is little short of amazing. For years it has lengthened the Church's arm, increased the Church's usefulness, rescued the perishing, cared for the dying, and snatched multitudes in pity from sin and the grave. And I plead with you to-day to send from this congregation an exceptionally liberal sum to strengthen the hands of those who are nobly working for the good of the masses in the slums of this great London, and practically acting out the petition in the Paternoster,

"THY KINGDOM COME."

THY WILL BE DONE.

" Thy will be done."—*Matt*. vi. 10.

THIS significant, profoundly reverent petition in the Paternoster invites consideration on two distinct planes of interpretation—
the Deistic and the Universal. On the Deistic
plane it implies intelligent, unswerving submission to the Divine order. On the Universal
plane it suggests active co-operation with the
benevolent purposes of the Creative Spirit of
the universe.

On the Deistic plane, which we will consider
first, the expression in the Paternoster, " Thy
will be done," is the fulfilment, the amplifica-
tion, and the elevation of all previous conceptions of man's relation to the hidden power within
ourselves that made and rules the world. There
has always existed the prevailing idea of an
irresistible Will behind phenomena. In all the
ancient religions, the conception obtained of omnipotent, irresistible Fate, the mysteries of whose
moral being were impenetrable. The Greeks per-
sonified the conception as Moira, from *moros*,
a lot. In Greek mythology the conception was

a near approach to a vague monotheism, for it predicated an over-ruling Unity, of an undefined kind, controlling even the Olympian deities. The Latins entertained the same conception under the name of Fatum, a word which has the significance of something uttered or spoken, a decree or ordinance against which the desires of the gods or the determinations of men were equally powerless. In later mythology these conceptions, both in Greece and Rome, were more definitely objectified. In Rome they were the Parcœ, the Fates ; in Greece the gods themselves were subject to the three daughters of the night : Clotho, the spinner of the thread of life ; Lachesis, who determined the lot in life of each one ; and Atropos, the inevitable. Clotho was represented with a spindle, Lachesis pointing with a staff to the horoscope of man on a globe, and Atropos with either a sun-dial, or an instrument with which to cut the thread of life.

It is interesting to trace the gradual spiritualizing of these dim anticipations of the Paternoster as the fulness of time for the Christian revelation was approaching. Sophocles and Plato came very near the truth with their conception of an omnipotent purpose governing the apparently accidental phenomena of life. But the Epicureans and the Stoics reverted to the older theory of either chance on the one hand, or blind fatality on the other. Then came forth the Christian revelation, and the Christian re-

velation absorbed, fulfilled, and purified the
vague thoughts of an expiring Paganism. The
new disclosure of the mystery of the Infinite
defined the nature of God as Spirit, the name of
God as Love, the relation of God to man as
Paternal. Jesus, the Eternal Word made flesh,
declared that man has but one Father, whatever
the accident of his earthly birth. He told us
that we were spirits begotten by the Father
Spirit, for awhile incarnated that we might be
educated for a higher sphere. He assured us
that the only Fatalism is the " shall " of God
when He says, " Ye shall be perfect "; the only
predestination, the predestination to conformity to
the image of the Ideal Man ; the only submission,
a tranquil trust in responsible Fatherhood and
a yielding co-operation with the processes of
Divine evolution. Thus He transcendentalized
Fatalism into Filialism ; He substituted trust
in Fatherhood for trembling belief in an omnipotent totality of forces. Fatalism had its
uses, and was capable of producing a splendid
disregard of danger and death. Filialism was
infinitely higher, as implying intelligent confidence in the purpose and power of a responsible
Parent Source. And, therefore, the Incarnate
Word took humanity by the hand, bid it mentally abstract itself from second causes, and gaze
into the Infinite and say, " Our Father which art
in heaven, hallowed be Thy name. Thy kingdom
come. Thy will be done."

The human mind is a stubborn pupil ; it has
ever a tendency to revert to the rudimentary.
In Mohammedanism, which in all probability
was a divinely prompted reaction from the gross
tritheistic conceptions which prevailed in the
Christian Church at the time of Mahomet, Allah,
though conceived as a personal God, virtually
became an inexorable law annihilating every
lower law and every movement of human volition. And, in spite of the daily recital of the
Paternoster, the old leaven of Fatalism worked
in the conceptions of Augustine and of Calvin,
and pervaded the philosophic conceptions of
Leibnitz and other necessitarians ; and Milton,
too, in spite of the Paternoster, seems to consider the problem insoluble, for he makes the
best of his fallen angels exercise their minds
fruitlessly on the controversy :

> Others, apart, sat on a hill retired,
> In thoughts more elevate, and reasoned high
> Of Providence, foreknowledge, will, and fate :
> Fixed fate, free-will, foreknowledge absolute,
> And found no end in wandering mazes lost.

Now, the question before us to-day is this :
Where do we mentally stand with regard to
these problems that Milton's fallen angels could
not solve ? " Fixed fate, free-will, foreknow-
ledge absolute." Does the Paternoster suggest
to us the peace-bringing solution, or are we,
too, " in wandering mazes lost " when we daily
repeat, " Thy will be done "?

What is the human will ? There is no exhaustive definition of the human will. Though there is hardly a great thinker from Descartes to Lotze who has not attempted a solution of the psychology of will, there is no consensus of opinion. In order that the petition in the Paternoster may not be unreal, it must imply that there is some resisting power in ourselves capable of contradicting and possibly delaying the Divine Will ; some volition that is executive when, after a struggle, we say, as the Perfect Elder Brother said in Gethsemane, " Not My will, but Thine be done." What is the secret of these apparently sundered wills of man and God ? I would state the case like this. I am, you are, we all are, Divine Spirit differentiated into separate self-conscious entities, each incarnated in a body evolved by a prolonged natural process from atoms of matter. Obviously, the All-Father has thus differentiated us, separated us off, for a glorious purpose, purposed before the world was, namely, that we may return to Him consciously, as perfected moral beings. Human life is, therefore, the divinely ordained education for an endless life with God. Now when you study mankind you perceive two prominent elements in this divinely ordained education—the Perfect Son was exposed to both of them—the one is suffering, the other is temptation.

The one, suffering, which is educative and

remedial, touches the question of volition only
in so far as it demands submission : the submission of Eli when he said, " It is the Lord,
let Him do as seemeth Him good "; the submission of David when he said, " I became
dumb and opened not my mouth, for it was
Thy doing "; the submission of our Lord when
He said, " If this cup cannot pass from Me
except I drink it, Thy will be done." No one
can have worked much amongst the suffering
poor without being astonished and rebuked by
the constant manifestation of this reverent submission. It is occasionally, in highly spiritual
souls, elevated above that sadness of resignation
which is implied in the well-known hymn :

> " If Thou shouldst call me to resign
> What most I prize, it ne'er was mine," etc.,

and it becomes an intelligent recognition of the
perfection of the Divine order, and then *fiat
voluntas tua* becomes a lifting of everything to a
higher plane, transmuting sadness into gain and
joy.

The other element in human education, namely,
temptation, would have no purpose unless it
appealed directly to volition ; for what is
temptation ? Temptation is a momentum in the
direction of the lower nature, by resistance to
which man gains in spiritual strength and becomes a moral being. Obviously, this momentum
implies a faculty of choice between alternatives,
and this faculty of choice has been misnamed

will.   I say misnamed, because a faculty of
choice is a characteristic of imperfection and
partial knowledge.   Perfect knowledge has no
faculty of choice.   If two cups are before me,
one poisoned and one harmless, one of which
I must drink, without the knowledge which
of the two is poisonous, I have an agonizing
faculty of choice ; if I know, I have no choice
in the matter.   Perfect knowledge obliterates
choice ;   the truth makes free by exterminating
choice.   God, for example, has no choice between alternatives ;   He has a will which can
only will right and truth.   When human nature
is at-oned, man will similarly have no choice ;
therefore, increasing in the knowledge of God
will be decreasing in the faculty of choice.

Now, to what extent do I possess this faculty
of choice, resulting from my want of knowledge,
which people are so fond of misnaming a will ?
It is well to consider this, because the crowning
sophistry of those who adhere to the blasphemy
of the endlessness of evil is that it is the result
of evil freely chosen and everlastingly persisted
in ; and this theory logically cancels omnipotence
and abolishes God.   The "will of God is our
sanctification ";   " God our Saviour will ($\theta\acute{\epsilon}\lambda\epsilon\iota$)
have all men to be saved."   Can anything be
conceived more absurd than that the Absolute,
the Omnipotent, can will anything impossible
of accomplishment ?   If man possesses a will,
in the sense that he can stiffen himself into ever-

lasting impenitence, then God does not possess
a will.

Does this limitation militate against or weaken
man's sense of responsibility ?   On the contrary,
it accentuates and illuminates it.   Responsibility
is ability to respond.   To what ?   To the promptings of that innate Divine faculty that sits in
judgment upon tendency.   All judgment is committed to the Son ;   that is, to the Logos or Divine
sonship within.   As we are dual, we have two
sets of tendencies, both hereditary, one from
the All-Father, the other from the human father.
When these make themselves felt, the Divine
faculty judges between them.   According to our
acceptance or rejection of the judgment our
characters are formed.   Each time the judgment
of the Divine faculty is accepted there is less
and less choice between alternatives ;   the right
becomes easier and easier ;   at last it becomes
automatic, and the will of God, which is our
sanctification, is done in our outer nature as it
is always done in the heaven of our inmost ;
and then we have really a free will, for the Son
of God nature has made us free to serve the
highest without choice or effort ;   and " if the
Son of God shall make you free, then shall you
be free indeed."

The same sequence obtains in the reverse
process.   If I reject the judgment of the Divine
faculty, and, in my want of knowledge, choose
the cup with poison in it, duller and duller

become the higher faculties, until at last my choice of the lower becomes automatic and I choose no more, and have become free to serve the lowest without choice or effort. And then ? The education of life is wasted, but the resources of Omnipotence are not exhausted. They were not exhausted in the case of Dives, though the alternative is alarming; and there ever remains the irrefragable prophecy, " Thy people shall be willing in the day of Thy power."

The conclusion which I draw from the Deistic plane of interpretation of this petition in the Paternoster is as follows :

(1) The will of God is the predestination of God embedded in my nature ; and the part and duty of the measure of volition I possess is to evolve what is involved in myself.

(2) The sphere of my nature in which the momentum is applied to provide the requisite resistance to stimulate this evolution is the mind ; for " out of the heart proceed evil thoughts," etc. ; in other words, desire is prompted by imagination.

(3) Therefore, I must watch those tendencies within me that produce desire, and when my Divine faculty condemns them I must, by forceful effort, change my thoughts so that action may be unborn. " Whatsoever things are true, holy, and pure," I must " think on these things."

(4) I have the right to appeal in every emer-

gency to the Divine force within me, which is
nothing less than the whole power of the kingdom of heaven; for Jesus tells me that the
Kingdom of God is within me, and I must throw
all this meaning into the petition in the Paternoster, and pray: "Thy will, O Father, be done
in this outer nature of mine, this false self, this
earth covering, as I know it is always done in
the mystic heaven of my inmost; for I know
that my real ego, my true life, is 'hid with
Christ in God.'"

One word upon the Universal plane of interpretation, on which plane the petition, "Thy
will be done," suggests active co-operation with
the ceaseless benevolent activity of the Creator
Spirit of the universe. The noblest expression of
this petition is in energy, not contemplation.
The more spirituality is read into it, the more
unweariedly will you fill every hour with effort
towards working out higher and more ideal
conditions everywhere. If ever the saying is
true, "*laborare est orare*," it is in transmuting
this petition into activity. On this plane of
thought your conception will not be Deistic;
you must not mentally separate God and will,
any more than you would mentally separate
God and love. Esoterically speaking, God does
not perform the mental act of willing; He is
Will, Absolute Will. When you say, "God
wills," it is another form of saying "God is";
for God is the central self-conscious Substance,

or Essence, or Intensity, the constraining law of whose being is Love. Esoterically speaking, God is not a " person " in the sense that we use the expression. If your mind requires the conception of individuality, it would be justifiable to say, " He is the universally diffused Individuality who is the uplifting life in all that is," and this conception is greater than personality. His self-definition given to Moses in the bush is, " I am." In the Hebrew Kabbala it is " Ain Suph," the endless, the boundless. That is, He is the totality of being behind universal life. This is, virtually, scientific as well as philosophical, because motion is the cause of causes in nature, and force is the cause of motion, and pressure is the cause of force ; and the greatest physiologists (W. B. Carpenter, Agassiz, Herschel, Richter, Newton, Sir William Hamilton) hold that behind the pressures that produce the motions of the universe is Will, and Will is God.

" Thy will be done," then, is far more than a mental aspiration in union with the activity of the Father Spirit ; it is active co-operation with every movement that tends to happiness, holiness, betterment. It is throwing yourself, your means, your services, your mental energy, into every organized effort to sweep away abuses, to remedy injustice, to effect the moral restitution of your fellow men. It is, in fact, to offer yourself as a vehicle, a *modus operandi*, to that Divine Spirit of evolution which, through the varied conditions, measures of capacity, and experiences of men, is working out an ultimate unity of life and perfection for all.

The passive, negative, acquiescing attitude has its usefulness, its great usefulness, on the Deistic plane, but it is not the highest on the spiritual plane, the plane of the Christian revelation of God. A patient, suffering from some sore disease, may mentally submit himself to the current of Fatherly love, and say, " Though He slay me, yet will I trust in Him "; " If it is His will that I should suffer and die, His will be done." Subjectively, the soul of that man is uplifted and purified ; it is a candidate for the love and tenderness of the Omnipotent Father Soul. But there comes on the scene the skilled surgeon, whose arduous labours and earnest devotion to duty have enabled him, under the improved conditions of modern surgery, wholly to remove by operation the disease from which this submissive patient is suffering, and restore him to health and usefulness ; and though the surgeon has not repeated the Paternoster, he has acted it, for the will of God is the activity of the Father-life that is ever originating, reproducing, healing, restoring ; and in the restoration of that patient, through the brilliant achievement of the surgeon, God's will is done.

Let us endeavour to lay it to heart. This interpretation of " *fiat voluntas tua* " would purge the world in a year ; but it will never be universal so long as Christian nations send armies to murder one another, and suffer jealousy and retaliation to guide their international relations; and political expediency, rather than principle, to rule their domestic legislation. All this is diametrically opposed to the benevolent current of the Father-Will.

But, individually, we may strive to remember that while submission to the Divine Will is the sublimest of mental attitudes, it does not justify evasion of the actions, duties, and demands of life, and that it becomes every possessor and repeater of the Paternoster not to stand idle in God's harvest-field, but to " work while it is day, for the night cometh when no man can work."

GIVE US THIS DAY OUR DAILY BREAD.

" Give us this day our daily bread."—Matt. vi. 11.

THE Paternoster, like the Decalogue, directs attention in its first half to the appropriate attitude of the human mind Godward. It asserts the Fatherhood, the Name, the Kingdom, and the Will of the Universal Soul, and teaches us to pray that the Fatherhood may be recognized, the Name accounted holy, the Kingdom and the Will become the kingdom and will of the inmost being of individual man.

In the second half, the Paternoster deals with those matters which relate to our conditioned state, as dependent on the Parent Soul for means of living, for emancipation from the consciousness of guilt, for a spirit of brotherly consideration for others, and for deliverance from evil.

The first of these, the means of living, comes before us for our consideration to-day ; and no petition in the Paternoster lends itself more completely to the dual principle of interpretation, the natural and the spiritual, than these words which our Lord has put into our mouths,

" Give us this day our daily bread." We will consider the petition on the Pauline principle : " first, that which is natural ; afterwards, that which is spiritual."

First, that which is natural. On this plane it is clear that the object of the petition is to emphasize and carry into daily life the Father aspect of the Universal Soul, which is the great disclosure of the Paternoster. It is to remind us that the Author of Life cares for life with an intensity proportioned to His responsibility, and that the receptive attitude in which this Divine Fatherliness should be acknowledged is recognized dependence upon Him who kindles the brain, nerves the arm, and sustains the lives of the children whom by thought-generation He has begotten.

Now, it would be easy to occupy the whole of this sermon with comments upon this reverent and tender plane of interpretation in its rudimentary sense, and relate instance after instance of exact and literal fulfilment of this petition, " Give us this day our daily bread." The confidence and simplicity of George Müller's daily prayer for his orphanage at Bristol, and the precise and specific answers which during many years he received, afford a striking illustration of special events following special supplications. Books could be filled, have been filled, with the experiences of those who with perfect confidence have asked for and received the exact sum of

16

money, or the precise measure of food, required
at a particular crisis. The matter-of-fact critic
hints at coincidence, and remarks that no record
is published of the instances when the affirmative
answer has not come to the prayer ; but, as Mr.
Spurgeon used to say, the coincidences are God's
coincidences, and every true believer tacitly
conditions his prayer with the proviso, " Not
my will, but Thine be done," knowing that the
Father is the best judge of the highest moral
interests of the petitioner. Amongst the simple
trusting poor in all lands, and under all forms
of faith, there is a ceaseless interchange between
man and God of petition and fulfilment on the
lines of the words of the Paternoster, " Our
Father which art in heaven, give us this day our
daily bread."

But I am addressing those who have never
been called upon to face that peculiar crisis.
Probably not one listening to me now has ever
been so situated as not to know from whence
their next meal would come. How then, without
a certain unreality, can they pray, on this
natural plane of interpretation, the petition,
" Give us this day our daily bread "? I reply
that the effect of this petition upon thoughtful
minds should be to direct their attention to the
complete dependence of man upon the Providence, the providing beneficence, of the Father
God. The selection of the word " bread," rather
than the abstract term " food," in the petition

significantly emphasizes this suggestion. There
is a curious analogy between bread and man
himself, in that both of them are, so to speak,
artificial products, wholly dependent, therefore,
upon the thoughtful activity of the producer.
What do I mean by saying that man is an
artificial product ? I mean that, in his totality,
he is not the direct result of evolution, which,
without the intervention of Him who hath made
us, would not take man higher than the anthropoid ape. The Universal Soul has enshrined,
in the inmost sanctuary of the body which He
has prepared by evolution, a Divine mystery,
and man is a combination of spirit, soul, and
body which does not exist in that proportion
and in that equipoise in anything else that
breathes. It is surely significant that as man
is thus an artificial product, so the main staple
of his food, the staff of life, is also artificial. No
edible cereals grow wild ; edible wheat is the
product of the artificial cultivation and careful
hybridizing of the wild cereal grass called
ægilops ovata. There is no trace of wheat having
ever evolved by natural selection from a cereal
grass, as the potato has evolved from the wild
solanum. In what age of the dim and distant
past man artificially produced the wheat plant
is unknown, but we do know that it was cultivated in China three thousand years before
the Christian era, and charred bread has been
discovered in the prehistoric lake dwellings.

This parallel artificiality of man and his bread
conveys a strong reminder that this earth life
is not man's home ; only his nursery, as it were,
or his temporary infant school, in which he has
been " made for a little while lower than Divine,"
that he may be educated for a higher sphere ;
and the petition, " Give us this day our daily
bread," is, in the mouths of those who have
never known a want of actual wheat or bread, an
acknowledgment of our complete dependence
upon the boundless power and love of Divine
Fatherhood.

Again, even if a man is a millionaire, he can
use this petition on the natural plane without
unreality ; for, apart from the facility with
which riches will make to themselves wings
and flee away, the special differentiation of man
from the animals other than man is his ability
intelligently to unite desire, and expression of
desire, in his approach to the Eternal. Obviously,
every need, every desire, is an unexpressed petition to the Immanent Life that uplifts the universe ; the rootlet of the tree feeling for water,
the open mouth of the fledgling in the nest of
the bird, act the petition, " Give us this day our
daily bread." But man is not man if thus he
lives, for man is sent into the world for a nobler
destiny than the rootlet of the tree or the bird
in the nest ; he is sent to learn the great disclosure of the Paternoster, namely, that God
is not an all-diffused blind power behind phe-

nomena, but a loving, responsible Parent Soul, who is welcoming to ever closer communion with Himself the children whom He has temporarily separated from Himself, as the child by birth is separated from its mother, that they may know Him as they could never have known Him if they had not been separated. Therefore, though He knows our necessities before we ask, and sends His rain both upon the just and the unjust, both on the prayerful and the indifferent, He welcomes our expressed petitions as evidence of our growing recognition of His relationship to us, as acknowledgment of our belief that He can and does and will modify phenomena, bend forces, and arrange natural sequences in response to the prayers of those who trustingly come to Him. And that we may give direct proof that we are greater than mere animal forms, and wiser than mere materialists, and more filial than mere fatalists, He encourages us daily to converse with Him in the words, " Our Father, give us this day our daily bread."

But, further, a man may be a multi-millionaire, and if he is an intelligent believer, and spiritually awakened, may throw intense meaning into the petition, " Give us this day our daily bread." His thought will expand ; he will see the Father Soul working in and moulding the symmetry of the universe ; he will place himself mentally into the midst of the wondrous chain of sequences upon which incidents depend ; his prayer will reach out and blend itself with the loving activity of the Master of the World ; he will think of the unexpected vicissitudes of international relations ; he will remember that if a hostile coalition deprived England of the command of the sea, the nation's daily bread would fail in a fortnight ; he will remember, again, how much during the winter depends, amongst the poorer classes, upon the price of the quartern loaf, and how much this depends upon the harvest. And there is literally no limit to the expansiveness of his prayer. When he says, " Give us this day our daily bread," his mind will be blending with the Universal Mind, and setting free influences that rule and govern the heart of things, that confer prudence and sagacity upon statesmen and diplomatists, that regulate atmospheric laws so that man may receive and enjoy the kindly fruits of the earth.

But there is yet deeper efficacy in the petition. The prayer is not " give me," it is " give us "; it is a witness to the solidarity of the race ; it is the affirmation that humanity is not stronger than its weakest link ; and such a prayer is a mockery if the petitioner is not labouring in the direction of its fulfilment. How can you labour to fulfil the prayer, " Give us this day our daily bread "? Not by indiscriminate almsgiving. If every one in this church sold all that they had to-morrow and gave it to the poor of London, the mischief

would be incalculable.   No ; to labour with the
prayer is to strive in season and out of season to
prevent the hideous waste in God's world of the
ample resources which He has bestowed.   It is
to provide daily bread for hungry millions by
inculcating habits of thrift, self-control, purity,
uprightness ;   it is to fight against the food-
wasting vices of the masses.   Surely it is a
curious inconsistency when professing Christians
pray daily, " Give us this day our daily bread,"
while they are fully aware that something like
a hundred million bushels of edible corn of
different kinds are destroyed every year in the
production of a commodity which is the prolific
cause of madness, pauperism, and degradation.
He who is labouring to minimize or remove
England's self-imposed curses can pray, with
a clear conscience, the petition, " Give us this
day our daily bread."

And, once more, and this is the last application that I will suggest on the natural plane,
this petition, if offered with intelligence and
spiritual insight, would prove a somewhat startling purifier of commercial life.   " Our Father,
give us this day our daily bread " deliberately
places the All Holy, unto whom all hearts are
open, behind every investment, every trade,
every occupation by which daily bread is gained.
Imagine asking the All-Father to bless an
investment which you know is filling gaols, peo-
pling almshouses, stocking asylums, multiplying

misery and degradation. Imagine the man who
goes forth to gamble on the Stock Exchange,
well knowing he has not the means to pay for
shares he has bought in hope of a rise in their
value, praying for a blessing on his venture.
Imagine solemnly praying this petition in connection with the frauds and shams and lies and
adulterations from which a considerable proportion of daily bread is made. The moral
standard of the commercial world would be
raised if the millionaire, as well as the pauper,
threw his whole heart into the petition : " Do
Thou, O Father, give us this day our daily
bread, and let what cannot come with Thy
blessing cease to come at all."

Let us now consider the scope and power of
this petition on the spiritual plane of interpretation, the plane of the real. Man does not
live by bread alone, for man is the spirit-child
of God and a sharer in His immortality. The
Lord in the wilderness was forty days without
the bread that nourishes the animal-human life ;
it is inconceivable that He was for a moment
deprived of the strength and sustenance of the
potent secret food of the Spirit. The inmost
meaning of the petition, " Give us this day our
daily bread," is indicated by the Greek word
translated " daily," namely, the word ἐπιούσιος.
It is clear that the evangelists recognized that
the Lord was lifting them to the highest spiritual
plane in this petition in the Paternoster, for in

all the copious and expressive Greek language
they could not find a word in which to embody
the spiritual idea that was conveyed to their
minds. They therefore made a word by com-
pounding the Greek word οὐσία, substance, with
the preposition ἐπί, above, or over. That compound word, ἐπιούσιος, has perplexed translators.
The so-called Authorized Version translated it
" daily." The revisers of the Authorized Version,
while retaining in the text the old translation,
have inserted in the margin the alternative
reading, " Our bread for the coming day "; a
strangely unenterprizing and narrow translation,
and wholly inconsistent with our Lord's admonition to take no thought for the morrow. Was it,
I wonder, ecclesiastical prejudice that made the
revisers unwilling to adopt the true translation
which is in the Roman Catholic Bible, called the
Douay Version ? In the Douay Bible the word
is translated " super-substantial." The Douay
Version is taken from St. Jerome's Latin translation, called the Vulgate, and the word in the
Vulgate is " supra-substantialis." St. Jerome
acknowledges his indebtedness to the classical
knowledge and spiritual insight of Marcella, and
here a woman's mind has penetrated more deeply
into the hidden meaning of the word than the
minds of schoolmen and theologians.

Pray, says our Lord, pray : " Our Father, give
us day by day our super-substantial bread ; give
us the bread of life ; pour into our spirits the

vital intensity of Thy supreme Spirit." On this
plane of interpretation there is nothing suppliant
in the petition. It is the confident demand of
those who recognize and claim their sublime
birthright as the offspring of the Infinite Spirit.
This petition, on the higher plane of interpretation, is a strong affirmation of sonship. It
implies that we have accepted the disclosure in
the invocation of the Paternoster and based our
lives upon it. It implies also that we have
swept away from it all the man-made limitations,
which cling to it like parasites, and have applied
it to universal humanity. It is a proclamation
of our aspiration to live and labour in the conscious recognition of this truth ; to develop
character from sonship, and not to it. Spiritually
understood, it should affect with surpassing
power the practice of the Christian life. The
dignity and responsibility attaching to such a
relationship should invigorate us for that struggle
with the lower nature by which alone we can
become moral beings. Struggle there must be ;
for a son is not begotten only, he has to be
made, and he is made by successive conquests
of the lower life by the higher. " Begotten, not
made " is true of all in eternal generation ; begotten and made is true even of the One Perfect
Son, the Incarnate Lord, who, because He was
a Son, " learned obedience." So, that we may
be made, that we may grow into that likeness
to which we are predestined to be conformed,

we claim our birthright in the Paternoster, and
say, " Give us, O Father, day by day, our daily
portion of super-substantial sustenance, that we
may grow up into Thee in all things."

What is this super-substantial daily bread,
which, as sons and daughters of the Most High,
we claim in the Paternoster ? Obviously, the
nature, the method, the measure of this secret
feeding upon God is, in our present condition of
knowledge, beyond and above definition. Like
the mystery of life itself, like the mystery of
growth, animal or vegetable, the process whereby
the Universal Spirit penetrates, vitalizes, uplifts
the differentiated spirit is beyond our perception.
But the broad leaf of the garden vegetable is
equally beyond our perception when it opens
thousands of microscopic mouths and eats the
sunshine, assimilating it so completely that it
can be recovered from the leaf in the form of
carbon. As the leaf lies open to the mid-day
rays its attitude is an unspoken prayer : " Give
us day by day our super-substantial food of
sunshine." When we have seen some failing
human body struggling painfully for breath,
and have witnessed the vivifying, exhilarating
effect of inbreathing oxygen gas, we have, I
suppose, seen a remote analogy of the feeding,
vitalizing power of the Spirit of the Father when
inbreathed by the differentiated human spirit.
The open mouth of the human spirit is the recognized sense of need, desire. " Blessed are

they that hunger and thirst "; the more the
human spirit hungers for God, the more will it
receive of the super-substantial food, the more
will its sonship grow, its character ripen, its
predestined conformity to the Ideal Specimen
increase.

One final thought. In what circumstances can
we, with the greatest directness, intensity, and
assurance, pray the prayer, " Give us this day
our daily bread "? The vital breath of the
Universal Spirit that feeds the individual spirit
is the Word, the Logos, the Self-utterance of
God, always in the world, but, in the fulness
of time, specifically embodied in Jesus, who gave
us the Paternoster. This Logos is, of course,
universally diffused, and, to the open eye,
discoverable everywhere, accessible everywhere.
But how rare are the open-eyed ! They were
not open-eyed to whom He said : " I am the
bread of life which came down from heaven ;
if any man shall eat of this bread he shall live
for ever. He that eateth Me shall live by Me."
Their eyes were closed. They said : " This is
a hard saying ; who can hear it ?" Is it a hard
saying still ? For two thousand years the Holy
Ghost has been teaching us since then, and is
it still a hard saying ? He knew that it would
remain a hard saying, that the open-eyed who
in powerful mental concentration upon the
all-diffusion of the Logos could feed on Him,
independently of local limits or special places,

would in every age be rare, very rare, even if they exist at all.   Therefore, in tender consideration for our finite apprehensions, He did localize into time relations, and space limitations, an authoritative manifestation of His all-inclusive Universal Presence.   He appointed a certain ceremonial, in the due performance of which, the mystic process of His Spirit feeding the human spirit should be absolutely guaranteed to man.   He connected the ceremonial with the familiar process of eating and drinking to strengthen the analogy, to appeal to the imagination, to assure us that as the morsel of bread, consecrated as a holy symbol, was assimilated by the human body and became part of it, so would His Spirit, at that supreme moment, blend with and feed and become part of the human spirit.   Just as the quivering luminous life-presence of the universe which was everywhere in every bush appeared to be localized for purposes of manifestation in the one bush that Moses saw, because Moses could not know that every common bush was equally afire with God, so the universally-diffused, ever-living, mystic presence of the Logos, which, as human minds cannot grasp boundlessness, is beyond the recognition of our ordinary consciousness, is specially guaranteed and focussed in the appointed external act of the celebration of the Blessed Sacrament.   And surely that is the moment, when we meet Him face to face, when we follow out literally His own directions, when with angels and archangels and all the company of heaven we laud and magnify His glorious Name : that is the supreme moment when with the greatest directness, assurance, and intensity we can offer the petition in the Paternoster :

" GIVE US THIS DAY OUR DAILY BREAD."

FORGIVE US OUR TRESPASSES.

" And forgive us our debts, as we forgive our debtors."—
Matt. vi. 12.

THOUGH no petition in the Paternoster would more encourage a thought-excursion into the esoteric and the universal than this, it is my intention to confine myself to those inferences which are on the perfectly obvious and natural plane of interpretation. For example, there are three separate Greek words used in connection with the Paternoster to convey the idea of sinfulness, upon the distinctions between which words thinkers might profitably exercise much of their intelligence. St. Luke, in his recital of the Paternoster, uses the word *hamartia*, missing the mark; St. Matthew, in the passage before us, uses the word *opheilemata*, debts; and in our Lord's commentary upon this petition, in the fourteenth verse, He uses the word *paraptomata*, transgressions. Each word has its peculiar associations, which yield numerous thoughts when examined on the spiritual and philosophical plane of interpretation. But for our present

purpose I will consider them all as simply
significant of what we ordinarily mean by sin,
namely, any act, or thought, or word, or deed,
voluntarily committed, which contradicts the
moral order of the universe.

Now, taking this petition upon the simple
and obvious plane of interpretation, four propositions suggest themselves :

(1) The source of forgiveness is God only,
and God is our Father.

(2) The nature of our Father's forgiveness is
not oblivion, but cure.

(3) The condition of our Father's forgiveness
is the possession of the forgiving spirit by the
son who is forgiven.

(4) The pattern of forgiveness is Jesus at
Calvary.

(1) The source of forgiveness is God only.
What a magnificent declaration was that of the
Scribes and Pharisees when they said, " Who
can forgive sins but God only ?" How infinitely
wider, deeper, and truer than· they were capable
of imagining when we add to it the revelation
of the Paternoster. " God only," " Dieu seul "
—the motto of the devoted *solitaires* of the
Convent of Biarritz. Nothing outside God ; not
one microscopic atom of all that is. Splendid
consolation for the wasting fever of the restless
heart of man ; everlasting antidote to the
pessimism inevitably engendered by the burden
of life. The All-wise Intelligence, whose revealed

name is Love, has caused us to be. Creatures of His hand, children of His love, minute rays of immortality from the central sun of His infinite mind we are; clothed for a while in atoms of matter, slowly struggling into consciousness, our birthright is in the boundless resources of His self-existent life; and to know that He is our Father, to know that there is One ever enwrapping us, wholly, absolutely, divinely responsible, and who knows all; knowing with perfect unerring certainty the origin, the influence, the weight of every downward tendency, temptation, predisposition in these lives of ours; this is peace. Buddha first expressed the sentiment; Madame de Stael turned it into an epigram, " To know all would be to pardon all." Man does not know all the mystery of his own nature, and has been bewildered by misrepresentations of his God. He often, therefore, cannot forgive himself or his fellow man. The Infinite Pity knows all, and, conscious of infinite responsibility, broods over us in this blundering babyhood of an earth life.

Nothing will prove a stronger, better stimulus to right doing than an increasing realization of the knowledge and responsibility of the eternal Fatherhood for every individual that He has caused to be. Lift up your hearts and believe it; strive earnestly so to yield the life that He may mould it according to His mighty purpose into fitness for His unveiled Presence; and throw

17

all this meaning into the petition, "Our Father, forgive us our trespasses."

(2) But let no man deceive us, for the process of the Divine forgiveness is cure, not good-natured oblivion : this is the second proposition. It is an awful as well as blessed thing to live ; we have a measure of freedom to misuse our education, and then the Father must cure us. Just as bodily disease is the result of minute living organisms preying on the vital tissues, and its essential remedy is the removal of the corrupted parts, and the impartation of higher, healthier life which will outlive and destroy the evil organism and make the body well, so sin is spiritual disease ; its result is to lower spiritual vitality, to paralyze the higher life ; and, when we are selfish and petulant and censorious and impure, it is our selves that we have injured. " He that sinneth against Me," said God, " wrongeth his own soul." The Father's forgiveness is curing us, saving us from the consequences of sin by removing the sin, with knife and cautery applied to the evil, and the impartation of a higher, purer, healthier life from Himself. The sacrifice of the Cross is not an artifice to enable a profligate to escape punishment because God is no longer affronted. Calvary is an everlasting manifestation of the missionary love of God, appealing to the hearts of men and assuring them that the way is open and the help is ready for the self-effort necessary to turn heavenwards.

No man ever escapes the consequences of his sins except as he is enabled through the life of God imparted to him to put away the sin itself ; and that imparted life of God will require of him that, sooner or later, the whole evil nature in man be surrendered to death. The Redemption of man consists in the fact that, by the energy of this new life imparted through the Christ of God, he is brought safely through the crisis of death unto sin into the life eternal that lies beyond it. He is saved, not from sin's penalty, but through it. Rest not, then, in any false or warped view of the Atonement ; do not cleave to some secret sin under the impression that God will overlook it at the last because Christ has done something instead of you. The Father loves you too well for that. His office is to cure ; His love is inexorable, and will shrink from no needful discipline. The will of God is our sanctification, and that Will must have its way even if in another age He has to re-melt in the eternal fire a character wilfully hardened in the mould of sin. All this is implied in " Father, forgive us our trespasses."

(3) Once more. The condition of forgiveness is the forgiving spirit. To this petition only did our Lord append a commentary : " For if ye forgive not men their trespasses, neither will your heavenly Father forgive your trespasses." Why did He append this commentary ?

The Paternoster disclosed a hitherto unre-

vealed relationship between God and man;
not a new relationship, remember; not a fresh
departure, but a revelation of the perpetual
attitude of the unchanging Father to His weak,
tempted, and erring children. Acceptance of
this newly revealed standing of the race, not by
cold intellectual assent to a credal proposition,
but by a vital act of the whole inward man,
would necessarily imply a growing likeness to
the Father, and a debt of love between man and
man of such magnitude that no personal affront
or offence could release man from the obligation
of seeking the offender's welfare from his heart.
The human conventional standard of forgiveness
which had been hitherto accepted as the Divine,
the *Lex Talionis*, was henceforth to be lifted
to the newly revealed standard of the Divine,
and its limitations and maxims swept away.
Adelaide Proctor's beautiful lines, comparing the
highest human love with the perfect love of
God, indicate the ideal :

> Kind hearts are here ; but yet the tenderest one
> Has limits to its mercy—God has none ;
> And man's forgiveness may be true and sweet,
> But yet he stoops to give it.   More complete
> Is love that lays forgiveness at thy feet,
> And pleads with thee to take it !   Only heaven
> Means crowned, not vanquished, when it says " Forgiven."

True, only heaven ; and the new revelation of
the Kingdom of Heaven is " within you "; so
the Paternoster binds us to extend to others
the same Divine pardon with which heaven

crowns us when from our hearts we cry, " Our
Father." And I should imagine that there is
not a single point in morals or theology concerning which we more habitually trifle with
our highest knowledge. When we consider the
misunderstandings and jealousies and discords
and sorenesses and sulkinesses that divide fami-
lies and split up churches and poison Christian
work, and then remember that each separate
individual, at least once daily, kneels down and
prays, " Our Father, forgive me my trespasses
as I am forgiving the trespasses of my brother,"
it is not difficult to account for the miserably
low standard of appreciation of the forgiveness
of God which exists amongst professing Christians. Our own standing in the full sunshine of
God's pardoning love depends upon our willingness to forgive ; not because our Father arbi-
trarily refuses His pardon apart from this
condition, but because the forgiving spirit can
alone realize the blessing of forgiveness. While
unforgiving, we are standing in self and not in
Christ ; the flower of our spiritual life has been
put away in a cellar out of reach of the sunshine
of communion with God ; we are already in the
hands of the tormentor, already in the prison of
an obdurate heart out of which we cannot go
till we have paid all our debt—our debt of love
to God and man. I know it is constitutionally
more difficult for some men to forgive than
others ; it seems not to be in their nature.

"Know you not," said James the Second to Argyle, "that it is in my power to forgive you?" "Yes, doubtless," replied Argyle, "it is in your power, but it is not in your nature."

Thank God, there is the blessed promise that the uttermost farthing shall be paid at last; that the might of God's Spirit shall break down the prison walls at last, and enable us from the new heart and the right spirit to love and forgive all. Meanwhile, to-day, while it is called to-day, it is well for us to remember that if we would not tell a lie in the Lord's Prayer, the detractors, the anonymous letter writers, the critics who wound our pride, the cowards who stab us in the dark, are to be forgiven as God in Christ has forgiven us; that is, heartily, without reservations; and it would be well often to take an inward look and pray earnestly: "That it may please Thee to forgive our enemies, persecutors, and slanderers, and to turn their hearts; we beseech Thee to hear us, good Lord."

(4) The last proposition is that the perfect pattern of forgiveness is Jesus at Calvary. The one profitable mental attitude in which to enter upon the solemn considerations of Holy Week and Good Friday is the clear realization that this suffering, sinless Being is not only an incomparable external model (He is that), but also the visible manifestation of a vital force working in each one of us which will ultimately conform us to the same character.

If ever the searching question, " What think ye of the Christ ?" is appropriate, it is when we mentally place ourselves at the foot of the Cross during the Church's annual Calvary Week. We have been taught " substitution " too long. It is well that we should learn " identification." In what did He differ from other men ? Without entering upon metaphysical subtleties, I reply : He differed from other men not in kind, but in degree.

Does that statement detract from His Divinity ? No ; it is to claim for Him the highest conceivable prerogative of Divinity. A theological conception of Jesus that would limit to His single Personality the out-breathing of the Creative Soul which is the attribute of humanity as a whole would be both unphilosophical and untrue ; but to say of Him that He was the one absolutely Perfect Specimen of the Creative Intensity Incarnate is to say of Him that He was " God of God, Very God of Very God," that " in Him dwelt all the fulness of the Godhead bodily," that " he that had seen Him had seen the Father," while it would not be to separate Him from the mass of humanity whom He solemnly and repeatedly claimed as His brethren. So when we mentally concentrate upon that human form nailed to the Cross, crushed beneath an unspeakable dishonour, we are gazing on One who is the complete embodiment of the moral nature of the unthinkable Absolute, and

therefore wholly Divine; and the objective
manifestation, in perfection, of that spirit or
quality of Sonship which is immanent in every
member of the race, and therefore wholly and
completely human. And in His profound, inexhaustible, world-embracing utterances from
the Cross we have given to us a self-revelation
of the attitude of the heart of God towards
humanity on the one hand, and a picture lesson
of those characteristics of perfect sonship which
are the natural outcome of the immanence of
the Logos, and to which we are predestined to
be conformed, on the other.

Is it not significant that the most remarkable
of these characteristics of perfect sonship should
have been a fulfilment in act of this petition of
the Paternoster? It seems to place it in the
forefront of Christian achievement. When He
had been hanging for three long silent hours
on the Cross—three hours of peculiar and intense
physical and mental agony—He justified for
ever by His own action the condition that He
attached to this petition in the Paternoster,
and manifested the crowning triumph of that
Divine Sonship which, for the benefit of His
human brethren, He had trained to perfection
and presented to the Eternal in the name of
the race. "Father, forgive them," He says;
"forgive these poor Roman barbarians, these
vacillating sheep fooled by their priests, who,
five days ago, would have made me a king and

now have hunted Me to My death. Forgive
Pilate, and the soldiers, and Judas ; forgive all
My enemies, persecutors, and slanderers, now
and for ever." No recorded words from the
lips of Him who spake as none other man
spake can compare with these. This is the
language of perfection, the most complete to
which man can attain ; and, as in our consideration of the Paternoster we have arrived
on the first day of the Holy Week at this special
petition, the test petition of Divine Sonship,
I suggest that it should be the prominent
thought of the Holy Week, and especially of
Good Friday. Let us recognize this word from
the Cross as our perfect assurance of the forgiveness of sins, our guarantee of the efficiency
of every absolution of the Church, our stimulus
to persevere in intercession for others, and,
above all, our safeguard against unreality when,
smarting perhaps under some injustice, we pray
daily in the Paternoster :

" OUR FATHER, FORGIVE US OUR TRESPASSES,
AS WE FORGIVE THEM THAT TRESPASS
AGAINST US."

LEAD US NOT INTO TEMPTATION.

" Lead us not into temptation, but deliver us from evil."—
Matt. vi. 13.

THE perplexity to reflective minds in this petition is expressed in the question : If temptation is common to man and part of his necessary education, why do we ask not to be led into it ? In answering the question, it will be necessary to condense the consideration of the petition.

What is temptation ? Temptation is a certain momentum, applied to the tendencies of our lower nature, calculated to provoke these tendencies to the perpetration of moral mischief, which momentum stimulates into activity the interior Divine nature whose resistance to the momentum builds up the human being into a true self-controlled son of God ; and the higher life, being thus stimulated, gradually conquers the lower life, until at last the true Divine ego becomes the master and the regulator of all human desires.

This process illustrates the extent to which man possesses a will. Man has no will in the sense of self-determinism, but he has the faculty of sitting in judgment upon his tendencies and discerning between them ; and as this discernment is more and more exercised in the direction of his higher tendencies, it becomes more and more automatic, till at last he has no will in the matter at all. When alternatives are presented to him, his will is so suffused, ensphered, blended with the higher Will, that he takes without effort the right course ; and now he is truly free, as the angels are free, as God is free— free to do the right without a struggle. The purpose of the momentum is fulfilled : " the Son of God has made him free, and he is free indeed."

Why is temptation necessary ? Because man, to become a moral being, as the Father has designed him, must be the author of his own goodness, which must be evolved from within, as a plant must be the author of its own flower, evolved from an interior germ which has prevailed over the hindrance of environment. To talk of a man being righteous because the righteousness of someone else is imputed to him is as irrational as to talk of a plant being perfect which has a blossom from another plant tied to it with string. Again : because an untempted human being is merely a grown-up child ; his potentialities are latent, untested, unevolved ; his goodness is negative, not positive ; his innocence is not morality, but inexperience. Again :

because man must be the creator of his own
character ; and character is the result of moral
decisions ; and moral decisions can only be made
under conditions in which the alternative of
an immoral decision was possible.

Consider. How did the unrivalled Elder Brother of the race attain His moral perfection ?
He was educated in the two schools through
which we all must pass, and to which I have
referred in a previous sermon : the school of
suffering and the school of temptation. The
school of suffering is not before us to-day ; but
most of us understand what Michael Angelo
meant when he said, "As the marble flies, the
image grows." "The First-born among many
brethren" graduated in the school of temptation. He was "in all points" tempted like as
we are. "In all points" does not, of course,
mean in the same sphere, but with the same
severity. The temptation of each man is conditioned by peculiarities arising out of personal
characteristics and circumstances. That which
is an agonizing temptation to one man has no
attraction for another. Jesus was "led up by
the Spirit to be tempted." "Led up by the
Spirit" thus are we all ; remember that fact
when next assailed by temptation. He was
"led up by the Spirit" to be tempted. I must
not enter into a full consideration of that allegorical epitome of the searching trial of the
Perfect Son which is called the Temptation of

Christ. That it is allegorical is obvious : first, because He records it Himself, and at a time when it was said, " Without a parable spake He not unto them"; secondly, because if some objective, exalted, personification, either such an one as Milton's Satan, or Goethe's Mephistopheles, or Noel Paton's glittering fiend, confronted Him, it would have been no effort to resist, and it would have negatived His identification with us, His brethren ; for that is not how we are tempted, and He was in all points tempted like as we are. No, the conception of Baron Munkacsy is the true one. In that striking picture, He is represented as alone, surrounded by the wild beasts, but otherwise alone, His head bent down in intense mental struggle. Obviously, the temptation to Him was to the pure, perfect beneficence of His human nature, to His pro-found pity for men, to His strong natural human patriotism. To have turned stones into bread would have mattered little, but it would have disqualified Him as our brother, because it would have been using a power for His own comfort which we do not possess. But to possess the kingdoms of the world through the agency of His purely human influence ; to win the homage of mankind by a descent through the air by psychic levitation, which would not require Divine power, into the crowded streets of Jerusalem ; to found a kingdom of heaven on earth ; to mould the thoughts and sway the

destinies of millions ; to abolish pain, disease,
death, moral and physical evil ; to soothe the
unrest and disorder of the whole universe : this
must have presented a well-nigh irresistible
temptation of agonizing intensity. He conquered, but only as you and I can conquer.
He chose the real instead of the phenomenal ;
the will of the Father instead of His own ; the
kingdom of heaven in hearts and not in earthly
peace ; and having been " in all points tempted
like as we are," and being now " with us always,
even to the end of the age," He is " able to
succour them that are tempted."

Now comes the question : If temptation be
thus essential to the formation of character,
and part of the regularized education of man,
why are we taught to pray not to be led into
temptation ? I cannot but think that this
petition is intended to inculcate self-distrust
and humble acknowledgment of weakness. It
is the instinctive cry of the alarmed human
conscience ; it is the recoil from the mental
attitude deprecated in the inspired warning,
" Let him that thinketh he standeth take heed
lest he fall "; it is like a child learning to swim
saying, " Lead me not out of my depth," while
knowing that being led out of its depth is the
one condition pre-requisite to learning to swim.
Then, again, our prayers must always be for
good results, and not necessarily for the circumstances that lead to the results. A child at

school might be sensible enough to know that chastisement, restraint, correction were for his ultimate good, but he would be quite consistent in praying against such circumstances as make correction necessary. We may be convinced that there are occasions when sickness may be better than health as a means of spiritual growth, but we should be quite justified in praying not to be led into illness.

Recognizing, then, my own infirm, imperfect, finite nature, and my instinctive recoil from conflict and pain and remorse, I acknowledge no contradiction between the vigorous spiritual injunction of St. James, " Count it all joy when ye fall into divers temptations," and the plaintive petition in the Paternoster, " Lead us not into temptation."

I think we stand on firmer ground when we finish the petition, and say, " Deliver us from evil." I have spoken so frequently and so fully, in many published sermons, upon the problem of the origin, the presence, the power of moral evil in the world, that I pass, without comment, many important phases of the subject. Though evil, as a concrete entity, does not exist except as a necessary foil and impulse to good, an essential condition of the recognition of good, it is impossible, and it would be inadvisable if it were possible, to soften the stern conception of evil that haunts the human conscience. It does not need the imagination of a Dante, it only needs the experience of life, to induce us to throw an eager pathos into the plea, " Our Father, deliver us from evil." It was Max Müller who first drew my attention to the appropriateness of the " serpent " idea in connection with the conventional personification of evil. The Sanskrit for serpent is *ahi*, the root of which is *anh*, to press together, to throttle. *Ahi* is the throttler, the choker. The Sanskrit word for evil is *anhas*, that which throttles. The celebrated Laocoon in the Vatican is the embodiment in statuary of what the ancients thought of evil. The English word anguish ; the Latin word for a snake, *anguis ;* the French word *angoise*, a cramped place, are all from the same root. Yes, evil is the throttler. When not resisted, it chokes the breath of God in the soul of man ; and, as we speak the word, there rises up the mental picture of the bitter anguish of this present earth ; its lazar-house diseases and base defilement ; its toiling, wearied, suffering multitudes ; its broken hearts, hopeless lives, and despairing deaths ; and, if we are not blinded by selfishness, however intensely we believe in the certainty of the final victory of the Overruling Power whose name is Love, we cry out, at times with a soul-agony unutterable, " Our Father, deliver us from evil."

It is, however, of the utmost importance, in praying this petition, to avoid faithlessness on the one hand, and to remember our mental

limitations on the other. We are not Deists ;
we are not praying to an objective, de-humanized,
despotic Creator ; we are speaking to the Abba-
Father. Our prayer must be qualified with the
reservation, Deliver us from what Thou seest
to be evil. Our apprehensions are imperfect ;
we are not always judges of what is evil ; sometimes, quite unconsciously, we say, " Evil, be
thou my good," and we mistake our good for
evil. Sometimes, when we pray, " Our Father,
deliver us from evil," we may be asking Him to
take from us what most we prize, and His answer
to the prayer is to dissect from us, at infinite
pain to ourselves, some heart-idol around which
the moral fibres of our being are closely bound.
Sometimes a crushing sorrow has come which
we have thought wholly evil, when in truth it
has been our Abba-Father answering our prayer ;
as it may have happened on the bodily plane
that one has gone to some physician with the
prayer, " Deliver me from this evil " of illness,
and he has delivered you, by serious operation,
from some morbid growth, or from a limb.

Again, it is well to remember the teaching of
Cyril of Jerusalem, and pray this petition
inwards, as a prayer to the Divine nature to
deliver you from the ruinous activity of the
sensuous nature. Blame has been cast on the
revisers for translating this clause " Deliver us
from the evil one." They are accused of introducing the devil into the Lord's Prayer. But

18

why the devil ?   There is no hint in the Greek
of this phantom that has dominated the religious
history of the world ; ἀπὸ τοῦ πονηροῦ is " from the
evil man."   There is no imaginable devil equal
in mischief and malignity to a thoroughly evil
man. The Satan of Milton is a far nobler
character than, say, a man who without pity
will lure unsuspecting simplicity to ruin ; or a
millionaire who, already wealthy beyond the
dreams of avarice, will make a corner in wheat,
and starve half the population of Europe into
bread riots to increase his personal gain. Such
men are devils, because within them are the
qualities which are ascribed to what is theologically called the devil. From such men we
pray in the Paternoster to be delivered.

But, still further, each one knows himself
better than he knows any other. As the Divine
light within increases, it enables you to gauge
the depths of the possibilities of evil in yourself ;
it creates an intense recoil from the memory
of things done and words spoken when conscience was benumbed or asleep, and in just
and severe self-condemnation you judge yourself, as St. Paul judged himself, " the chief of
sinners."

Augustine, powerful as his mind was, is
responsible for not a little misleading theology,
but we owe to his self-knowledge and insight
the best translation of this petition in the
Paternoster : " Lead me not into temptation,
but delive me from that evil man, myself."

Finally, if we desire a test as to the growth of the Divine sonship, of which this petition is an outcome, we shall find it in a rigid analysis of our attitude towards, first, ourselves, and, secondly, towards the humanity of which we are a part. The old Persian fable of the pig and the sheep that fell into the ditch, and while the pig revelled in the mire the sheep agonized in the sense of uncleanness, is an apt illustration of the first. Does it agonize you to fall? Though to fall is not always to fail, does it torture you? Is your cry of remorse the voice of your deepest knowledge of yourself? Then it is well; the greatness of the Divinity within you is the measure of your horror at having fallen into the mire; the intensity of your self-condemnation is an evidence of the increasing antagonism existing within you between the Divine nature and whatever is antagonistic to its growth. Go on praying, " Our Father, lead us not into temptation, but deliver us from evil "; thou art not far from the kingdom of heaven.

As to the second test, your attitude towards the humanity of which you are a part: remember, the Paternoster is based on the one-ness of the race. It is not " my " Father, it is " our " Father. The evil in another, the fall of another, is our evil, our fall, in him, ever necessitating the prayer, " Deliver us from evil." The master-piece of evil is the non-recognition of evil. To

18—3

look down into the depths of distress and not
to care ; to live in the midst of records of misery
and crime and to be unconscious of any responsibility ; never to raise a hand or a voice to
make it easier for the masses to do right ; to
encourage and to strengthen the position in
the nation of ruinous, soul-destroying vices,
this is to make the repetition of the Paternoster,
" Lead us not into temptation, but deliver us
from evil," either a deliberate untruth or an
unconscious blasphemy.

I say it advisedly, no man can honestly pray,
" Our Father, lead us not into temptation, but
deliver us from evil," who never makes an
attempt to lead his brother out of temptation
and to deliver him from evil. For I read in
God's immortal literature, in Prov. xxiv. 11, 12 :
" If thou forbear to deliver them that are drawn
unto death ; if thou sayest, Behold, we knew
it not ; doth not He that pondereth the heart
consider it ? and He that keepeth thy soul,
doth not He know it ? and shall not He render
unto every man according to his work ?"

FOR THINE IS THE KINGDOM.

"For Thine is the kingdom, and the power, and the glory, for ever and ever. Amen."—*Matt*. vi. 13.

ALL are aware that this majestic ascription of universal dominion to the Creative Soul is omitted from the Revised Version. The translators have placed a note in the margin to this effect: "Many authorities, some ancient, but with variations, add, "For Thine is the kingdom," etc. Personally, I am not prepared to lose this noble doxology; and the fact that the words are not included in the oldest MSS. does not, to my apprehension, touch the question of their inspiration. I grant that it suggests the possibility of words being ascribed to our Lord, and to the writers of the New Testament, which were not spoken by Him or written by them. I feel little doubt that there are some such passages which are not genuine Logia, or sayings of the Lord Jesus. I should, for instance, be very unwilling to accept as a fact that He said, "All that came before Me were thieves and robbers." It is not like Him, and it would be a denial of the supreme truth that the great

thinkers who preceded Him were vehicles, trans-
mittors of the Logos, which was embodied in
perfection in Him.

But even this does not touch the question of
inspiration. What is inspiration ? To answer
the question, it is well to bear in mind the three
axioms which I have pressed you to consider
as lying at the root of the Christian revelation :
namely, (1) the universal responsible Fatherhood
of the Unconditioned Intelligence ; (2) that one
life, one love, one intelligence pulses through
all that is ; (3) that the Lord Jesus is the unit
of the universe, and the manifestation in perfection of a Divine Sonship which is the attribute of humanity as a whole. And when you
have laid down these axioms, you at once see
the universality of the principle called inspiration ; the certainty that inspiration can only
be apprehended by inspiration ; and that inspiration is from within outward ; the stirring of
the immanent Divine nature seeking to express
God ; and that the term cannot be limited to a
book or a literature. Inspiration is met, judged,
discerned, apprehended by inspiration, and by
nothing else ; and where the spiritual and rational
faculties have become so far matured as to
enable us to discern between more or less
imperfect expressions of truth, there will be no
difficulty in determining the relative value of
such expressions ; and this principle of determining inspiration by the acceptance of the

inspiration within is of priceless value, as it demands no critical faculty, research, or learning, and is more certain than all these combined, as it is " deep calling unto deep."

Now, as regards this later addition to the Paternoster, transcribed, in all probability, from a liturgy of the early Church, there need be no difficulty in accepting the words as inspired. They kindle within us immediately the response of the Divine fire ; they penetrate to our own indwelling Divine natures ; we recognize them as profoundly true, whoever first spoke or wrote them.   Moreover, they are Scriptural, as spoken of old time by King David (1 Chron. xxix. 11) : " Thine, O Lord, is the greatness, and the power, and the glory, and the victory, and the majesty : for all that is in the heaven and in the earth is Thine ;   Thine is the kingdom, O Lord, and Thou art exalted as head above all."

In accepting, then, this doxology as wholly inspired, though not discoverable in the earliest MSS., let us consider, first, how grandly it asserts the irresistible omnipotent over-rule of the universal responsible Creative Spirit ;   how utterly it obliterates from the mind the bene- volent, but feeble, despot invented for us by the authors of so-called " plans of salvation " and systems of theology.   They may be, they are, useful on the rudimentary plane ; but the Eternal Universal Spirit rules through all, in all, and over all.   He works slowly, and through processes which our apprehension is at present too limited to grasp ; but He works irresistibly, and creaturely self-will is compassed about on all sides by the Eternal Love. The measure of volition, entrusted to man to enable him to be built into a moral being, fills the world with apparent and temporary disorder. This educative nightmare necessarily appears to be antagonistic to God's will ; and so, in a sense, it is ; but the whole mystery of evil and all its crossworking purposes are completely under the over-rule of the Omnipotent. There can be no such thing as the finality of evil. When the process of training by contrasts is past, when the last moral being has struggled and conquered, the painful educative illusion called evil will pass like a cloud before the sunshine, for " His is the kingdom, and the power, and the glory, for ever and ever."

Secondly, how illimitable is the dignity that this doxology ascribes to humanity ! When we pray the petitions in the Paternoster, especially the petition " Thy kingdom come," we are not praying for what is not yet, but may be, but for the realization of that which actually is, and is for us, when we are prepared to receive it. The Father's kingdom, His power, and His glory are for ever ours, because they are His. All that has been, is, and is to come are eternal, as Divine realities, in Him ; and as unfulfilled potentialities in His offspring. Every one born into this world, or into any other world, is an heir of the All-Creating Spirit, projected by an orderly sequence of descent from God into matter ; a joint heir with the Perfect Son, only awaiting his spiritual majority to enter upon and enjoy his hereditary possession. All knowledge, all truth, all goodness, in the future as in the present, are the evolution of that which is everlastingly, though not as yet in fulness to us. If man, as the crown of existent life, has been evolved through lower organisms, it is certain that in his as yet unrealized perfection he has always subsisted at least, if not existed, in some form or other, whether as more spiritual in the fire mist of the planet, or in more material form in some distant realm of the universe.

Men do not gather grapes of thorns or figs of thistles ; still less can mind, with all its powers and capacities, be evolved from what is mindless. We were God's children before we were clothed upon with mortal flesh. Ours is the kingdom, because it is our Father's. Ours is the power, because to the Perfect Elder Brother has been given " all power both in heaven and on earth." Ours is the glory ; for as the Father's glory is not in and for Himself, but for the children, that they may bring forth much fruit of love and righteousness, so the pulsation of His glory, His *doxa*, is the driving power behind evolution which must eventuate in the expulsion of corruption and mortality. As the Father is infinite, so must be the offspring, though finited in time.

> To roll and sweep and bind
> Suffice for Nature's part ;
> But motion to an endless end
> Is needful for the heart.

Let me point out, thirdly, that this doxology fortifies us with the guarantee that our lives are ensphered, permeated, by that threeness in unity which has been revealed as the order of thought in which we are bidden to conceive the All-producing Intelligence, and which is called the Trinity. " The kingdom, the power, and the glory " are terms that suggest an analysis of the nature of God. You may attribute the words almost as you will to each of the three Subsistences, but " the kingdom " is the Logos, the Self-utterance of God, evolving all that was involved in the first Source—the hidden Majesty that produces, advances, develops, rules all organisms, ever working out higher and higher forms of life. " The power " is the Holy Ghost, the outflowing life of the Logos and the Parent Source ; secret, unerring, constant, acting on human spirits as the power of gravitation acts on the planet. " The glory," the *doxa*, is the Unthinkable Absolute, the Cause of causes, ever unknown, but becoming knowable by becoming Father, and becoming Father by entering into spheres external to His essence and moulding them after His likeness. In the midst of this hidden Majesty of over-rule, power, and creative activity, our lives are placed ; from it they can

never escape; and though an open field is given
to us for the display, to our infinite sorrow, of
our creaturely wills; to know that we can never
escape from the Fatherly purpose is to fill the
heart with a profound sense of rest and security.

But, lastly, this doxology appears to me to
appeal with surpassing power to our practice.
It suggests the strongest conceivable motive to
live with our whole energies the higher life.
This revelation of the inseverability of the
human and the Divine casts a terribly deep
shadow over our failures, and stimulates the co-
operation of the Divine part of our nature. It
implies a relationship to the Eternal so close
and intimate that when we surrender self to the
lower appetites we are guilty of a shameful
disloyalty, we are dethroning the Divine within
us. A millionaire preferring to live in a work-
house is a monument of wisdom compared with
a believer in this doxology who deliberately lives
to pamper his lower self, preferring the indulgence of the appetites he shares with his dog, to
the development of the noble, the God-like, the
aspiring which he shares with God as being a
" joint heir with the Christ." Thus has the Lord
provided for us in the Paternoster not only perfect consolation, but cogent warning. The nature
life must yield to the evolution of the Divine
germ; and this yielding must be the conscious
act of the individual volition. We have the
power to live in opposition to our Father's ideal;

if we had not, we could never become moral
beings ; and when we repeat the noble words
of the doxology, it should say to each one of us :
Thou offspring of God, rise out of the nightmare
of the unreal ; unfold thy hidden capacities ;
avert thy mind from thy infirm, querulous,
temptable humanity ; curb appetite, subdue
temper, crush back angry words, force thy life
to rise, brace thy energies in opposition to all
that holds thee down ; fight with unwearied
courage against all that holds others down ;
raise thy voice against evils that undermine
the morality of the commonwealth and make
hells on earth where Edens ought to be. Thou
canst ; for, as a joint heir with the Christ, " thine
is the kingdom, and the power, and the glory, for
ever and ever."

There is one more word : the word " Amen."
The last word in the Paternoster, in the version
we habitually use, is the utterance of perfect
assurance. Ἀμήν is the last stroke of the
hammer that clinches the nail. *Amun* is the
old Hebrew word for faith ; its Greek equiva-
lent, ἀμήν, is the introduction to the most important of our Lord's recorded sayings. " Verily,
verily " is "Ἀμήν, ἀμήν." It is not " So be it,"
or " So let it be," but " So it is," or " So it must
be." Yes ; so it is, so it must be. There is
no logical halting-place between the assurance
that " His is the kingdom, and the power, and
the glory " and the dreary conclusion that blind

force moulds matter in obedience to law, and that we men are the highest products of a chance.

So, *sursum corda*, lift up your hearts. The victory is not yet ; we have, perchance, much still to endure ; but the end is certain. And when lips are trembling, and evil seems victorious, and heartstrings are snapping, look up into the Infinity ; challenge the Creative Soul with His own divinely revealed declaration of love, power, and responsibility in the Paternoster. Say to Him :

" OUR FATHER WHICH ART IN HEAVEN, THINE
IS THE KINGDOM, AND THE POWER, AND
THE GLORY, FOR EVER AND EVER.
AMEN."

BY THE SAME AUTHOR.

SECOND EDITION.   In crown 8vo, cloth, gilt lettered.
Price 5/-.

FEELING AFTER HIM.

SERMONS PREACHED, FOR THE MOST PART, IN WESTMINSTER ABBEY.

(SECOND SERIES.)

EXTRACT FROM PREFACE.

The preacher does not assume to provide a clear solution to the weary problems which surround human existence ; he merely records the experience of a heart "feeling after Him" with an unshakeable conviction that the responsible Creative Spirit is, by virtue of His omnipotence, under obligation to effect, here or elsewhere, the moral perfection of all that He has caused, by thought-generation, to be.

" Instinct with pathetic sympathy for the social side of life, interluded with poetical quotations and story-lore, deftly handled, the Archdeacon's sermons are characterised by light and freshness, and an earnestness, even to enthusiasm, of devotion to the good of his fellow man."—*Family Churchman.*

" When Archdeacon Wilberforce comes to practical exhortation he is splendid ; earnest, forcible, and fearless.   Several of the sermons have special reference to recent national events. The book has much to commend it."—*Aberdeen Free Press.*

" These eighteen sermons contain brilliant and sometimes daring thoughts, expressed in eloquent language, so that our interest is excited, even when our consent is not gained."—*The Guardian.*

" Exceptionally able, thoughtful, vigorous, and inspiring."—*—Weekly Leader.*

" What a feast for reflective minds the whole volume provides ! "—*Christian Commonwealth.*

" The sermons are eloquent and inspiring, and made interesting and instructive by apt illustrations from life and literature."—*Scotsman.*

ELLIOT STOCK, 62, PATERNOSTER ROW, LONDON, E.C.

Tastefully printed in crown 8vo size, and bound in cloth, gilt.
Price 3/6.

LIGHT ON THE PROBLEMS OF LIFE.

SUGGESTIVE THOUGHTS GLEANED FROM THE TEACHINGS OF THE VEN. ARCHDEACON WILBERFORCE.

By M. B. ISITT.

" This is the sort of book one is always glad to have at hand, and will certainly be of great service and help to the despondent and doubting."—*Whitehall Review.*

" It will be found that the compilation reflects earnest care and intelligence."—*Globe.*

" These extracts have been very carefully and thoughtfully selected. All those who know Archdeacon Wilberforce's books will enjoy them."—*Church Family Newspaper.*

" Dr. Wilberforce illuminates all he touches, and one is fairly won by his tenderness, courage, and skill. The work will prove a rich blessing and high inspiration to all who devoutly study it." —*Methodist Sunday School Record.*

" One may take up the book at any time and from its pages get comfort, advice, or admonition. A volume of considerable interest."—*St. Andrew.*

" An exceedingly interesting collection of thoughts upon great subjects gleaned from the writings of Dr. Basil Wilberforce."— *Liverpool Daily Post.*

" We have here the robust thought of a strong mind and a sympathetic spirit. To read such a book is a moral and spiritual tonic."—*Sunday at Home.*

" The selections have been made with care and judgment "— *Oxford Chronicle.*

" We can heartily commend these pages. Occasionally we get a great truth put in a remarkably brief and memorable way."—*Scottish Review.*

" These broad-minded heart-searching sentences should prove stimulating and helpful to a wide circle."—*New Age.*

ELLIOT STOCK, 62, Paternoster Row, LONDON, E.C.